D0667148

The Quotable Politician

Edited by
William B. Whitman

THE LYONS PRESS
Guilford, Connecticut
An imprint of The Globe Pequot Press

To buy books in quantity for corporate use
or incentives, call **(800) 962–0973**
or e-mail **premiums@GlobePequot.com.**

Copyright © 2003 by The Lyons Press

ALL RIGHTS RESERVED. No part of this book may be reproduced or transmitted in any form by any means, electronic or mechanical, including photocopying and recording, or by any information storage and retrieval system, except as may be expressly permitted in writing from the publisher. Requests for permission should be addressed to The Globe Pequot Press, P.O. Box 480, Guilford, CT 06437.

The Lyons Press is an imprint of The Globe Pequot Press.

10 9 8 7 6 5 4 3 2

Printed in the United States of America

ISBN 978-1-59228-132-9

Library of Congress Cataloging-in-Publication data is available on file.

Contents

Introduction

When The Lyons Press asked me to compile this book of political quotations, I jumped at the chance. I've always been fascinated by political rhetoric, and it seemed like a match made in heaven. Being cagey, however, like most writers (and all bureaucrats), I warned my editors that this would surely be a difficult task, demanding huge amounts of hard work, research, and critical judgment. I never told them what I'm now telling you—that for many years I collected quotations for a living.

Yes, folks, for about thirty years, as an American diplomat stationed in Washington and overseas, I diligently tracked the speeches, off-the-cuff remarks, and pontifications of foreign leaders, ranging from the president of Bolivia to the Pope to Tito. And to tell the truth, it wasn't nearly as much fun as working on this book. Alas, unlike the quotations I've selected for you, most of those I pored over and analyzed for the State Department were hopelessly pedestrian, covering heart-stopping subjects like agricultural reform in the Amazon basin and the cement production goals of Yugoslavia's umpteenth five-year plan. I'm happy to say that you'll find none of those boring remarks in this volume.

Statesmen, diplomats, and politicians understand something many private citizens do not—that words have real consequences and impact. This truth is evidenced in the statements of many of our finest American leaders. While I was stationed abroad, wading through those dreary speeches, my counterparts in the Italian or Bolivian embassies in Washington had the much more thrilling job of reporting back to their governments on the rousing and inspiring speeches made by John F. Kennedy, which served as a clarion call summoning an entire generation to public service as Peace Corps volunteers, Justice Department lawyers, and in my case the Foreign Service.

A generation earlier, during the Nazi air attacks on London, diplomats and anyone with a radio could tune in to hear, through the crackling of the shortwave, Winston Churchill's history-making speeches rallying the British people in their "darkest hour." And throughout the depths of the Great Depression and later in wartime, Franklin Delano Roosevelt's fireside chats similarly reassured countless Americans fighting first their own economic despair and then a devastating world war.

Unfortunately, in putting this book together, I found it increasingly difficult to discover recent quotes with the same degree of political incisiveness, wit, and strength that characterized American political discourse during the country's first two hundred years. With the exception of Ronald Reagan, who often graced the public with a well-timed, clever phrase, the past forty years have proved to be more and more challenging for American quotemeisters and connoisseurs of the *mot juste*. As one reporter put it, "The days of the Gettysburg Address are long gone."

Many observers blame what Senator John McCain calls "the impoverishment of our political discussion" on television's demands for the easily digestible and often content-free sound bite, and the public's increasingly short attention span for following increasingly complex issues. Others point to the harsh rhetoric often found on talk radio and, from the left, the deadening impact of political correctness as additional factors inhibiting rational political discourse in the United States. The pervasive use of e-mail and chat rooms and the premium those forums place on bare-bones, frill-free communication will no doubt worsen the situation.

In this book I've tried to combine the eloquent, insightful, and inspirational sayings that have moved people since the earliest days of recorded political activity with examples of the wit, irreverence, and, yes, cynicism that have enlivened political commentary (and many an after-dinner speech) over the centuries. I divided the book into chapters that group the quotations into general themes, including one on Washington, D.C., which is the target of many a political jibe, even by those of us who live there and like it.

In chapter 6, "The Presidency," and chapter 7, "Congress," you'll find some of my favorite quotes—many of them impertinent—about our First Citizen and our nation's lawgivers. From Roman politician Petronius Arbiter we learn that Washington's chronic practice of forming special committees and reorganizing to give the appearance of being on top of new national security and other challenges is far from new and has in fact been going on since 210 BC. Predictably, the chapter on power, which is what politicians thirst for, turned out to be one of the longest, while that on war, with its Churchill quotes, is perhaps the most inspirational.

Since I started this project, friends have asked about my favorite quote, and I invariably (and modestly) respond that this book contains so many witty and pithy sayings, it's almost impossible to single out just one. But in view of my former profession, I'm personally partial to Adlai Stevenson's definition of a diplomat's life, which, he said, "is made up of three ingredients: protocol, Geritol, and alcohol." Pretty astute, that Adlai.

1

Defining Politics

The bedfellows politics makes are never strange. It only seems that way to those who have not watched the courtship.

MARCEL ACHARD, FRENCH DRAMATIST AND JOURNALIST (1899–1974)

Practical politics consists in ignoring facts.

HENRY BROOKS ADAMS, AMERICAN HISTORIAN AND AUTHOR (1838–1918)

Politics: the art of keeping as many balls as possible up in the air at one time—while protecting your own.

SAM ATTLESEY, TEXAS JOURNALIST (1946–2003)

Politics is show business for ugly people.

PAUL BEGALA (1962–), POLITICAL CONSULTANT FOR FORTY-SECOND
U.S. PRESIDENT BILL CLINTON

Politics, *noun*. A strife of interests masquerading as a
contest of principles. The conduct of public affairs for
private advantage.

AMBROSE BIERCE, AMERICAN AUTHOR AND SATIRIST (1842–1913)
THE DEVIL'S DICTIONARY

Politics is supposed to be the second-oldest profession. I have come to realize that it bears a very close resemblance to the first.

RONALD REAGAN, FORTIETH U.S. PRESIDENT (1911–)

Politics is the art of the next best.

OTTO VON BISMARCK, GERMAN CHANCELLOR (1815–1898)

Politics: where fat, bald, disagreeable men, unable to be candidates themselves, teach a president how to act on a public stage.

JIMMY BRESLIN, AMERICAN NEWSPAPER COLUMNIST (1930–)

Politics is made up largely of irrelevancies.

DALTON CAMP, CANADIAN POLITICAL COLUMNIST (1920–2002)

The first mistake in public business is the going into it.

BENJAMIN FRANKLIN, U.S. WRITER AND STATESMAN (1706–1790)

The end move in politics is always to pick up a gun.

RICHARD BUCKMINSTER FULLER, AMERICAN ARCHITECT, INVENTOR
(1895–1983)

Politics is the art of the possible.

OTTO VON BISMARCK, GERMAN CHANCELLOR (1815–1898)

Politics is not the art of the possible. It consists in choosing between the disastrous and the unpalatable.

JOHN KENNETH GALBRAITH, AMERICAN ECONOMIST AND AUTHOR (1908–)

Those who say religion has nothing to do with politics do not know what religion is.

MOHANDAS GANDHI [MAHATMA], INDIAN NATIONALIST AND SPIRITUAL LEADER (1869–1948)

Politics is too serious a matter to be left to the politicians.

CHARLES DE GAULLE, FRENCH GENERAL, STATESMAN, AND PRESIDENT (1890–1970)

It is a curious fact that when we get sick we want an uncommon doctor. . . When we get into a war, we dreadfully want an uncommon admiral and an uncommon general. Only when we get into politics are we content with the common man.

HERBERT HOOVER, THIRTY-FIRST U.S. PRESIDENT (1874–1964)

There are no morals in politics; there is only expedience. A scoundrel may be of use to us just because he is a scoundrel.

VLADIMIR LENIN, RUSSIAN REVOLUTIONARY AND FOUNDER OF BOLSHEVISM (1870–1924)

Politics have no relation to morals.

NICCOLO MACHIAVELLI, ITALIAN STATESMAN AND POLITICAL PHILOSOPHER (1469–1527).

Politics is an excellent career, unless you get caught.

ROBERT HALF

Politics is the art of looking for trouble, finding it, misdiagnosing it, and then misapplying the wrong remedies.

GROUCHO MARX, AMERICAN COMEDIAN (1890–1977)

Being in politics is like being a football coach. You have to be smart enough to understand the game, and dumb enough to think it's important.

EUGENE MCCARTHY, FORMER DEMOCRATIC SENATOR OF MINNESOTA (1916–)

The essentials of Canadian politics are few: the system needs enough good men to make it work and enough fools to make it interesting.

DALTON CAMP, CANADIAN POLITICAL COLUMNIST (1920–2002)

Turn on to politics, or politics will turn on you.

RALPH NADER, AMERICAN POLITICAL FIGURE AND REFORMER (1934–)

Crime does not pay . . . as well as politics.

ALFRED E. NEUMAN, FICTIONAL PHILOSOPHER, *Mad* MAGAZINE

Politics is the skilled use of blunt objects.

LESTER B. PEARSON, CANADIAN PRIME MINISTER (1897–1972)

Politics is just like show business. You have a hell of an opening, coast for a while, and then have a hell of a close.

RONALD REAGAN, FORTIETH U.S. PRESIDENT (1911–)

All politics are based on the indifference of the majority.

JAMES "SCOTTY" RESTON, AMERICAN JOURNALIST, PULITZER PRIZE
WINNER (1909–1995)

I've always said that in politics, your enemies can't hurt you, but your friends will kill you.

ANN RICHARDS, FORMER DEMOCRATIC GOVERNOR
OF TEXAS (1933–)

Politics is for people who have a passion for changing life but lack a passion for living it.

TOM ROBBINS, WRITER AND SATIRIST (1936–)

If you ever injected truth into politics you'd have no politics.

WILL ROGERS, AMERICAN HUMORIST (1879–1935)

Politics is perhaps the only profession for which no preparation is thought necessary.

ROBERT LOUIS STEVENSON, SCOTTISH AUTHOR (1850–1894)

What's real in politics is what the voters decide is real.

UNKNOWN

Politics is the art of preventing people from busying themselves with what is their own business.

PAUL VALÉRY, FRENCH POET AND ESSAYIST (1871–1945)

Politics in America is the binding secular religion.

THEODORE H. WHITE, AMERICAN POLITICAL WRITER (1915–1986).

Politics interests people who don't know how to make money or love.

ANONYMOUS

Politics is about who wins and loses. The rest is of marginal interest.

SEAN WILENTZ, PRINCETON HISTORY PROFESSOR AND WRITER (1952–)

In politics, strangely enough, the best way to play your cards is to lay them face upwards on the table.

H. G. WELLS, BRITISH AUTHOR (1866–1946)

Nothing is so admirable in politics as a short memory.

JOHN KENNETH GALBRAITH, AMERICAN ECONOMIST AND AUTHOR (1908–)

———

Politics is war without bloodshed while war is politics with bloodshed.

MAO ZEDONG, CHINESE LEADER AND DICTATOR (1893–1976)

I adore political parties. They are the only place left to us where people don't talk politics.

OSCAR WILDE, IRISH PLAYWRIGHT, AUTHOR (1854–1900)
"AN IDEAL HUSBAND"

Politics is, as it were, the gizzard of society, full of grit and gravel, and the two political parties are its two opposite halves—sometimes split into quarters, it may be, which grind on each other.

HENRY DAVID THOREAU, U.S. PHILOSOPHER, AUTHOR, NATURALIST (1817–1862)
"LIFE WITHOUT PRINCIPLE"

Politics is not an exact science.

OTTO VON BISMARCK, GERMAN CHANCELLOR (1815–1898)

———

Politics is not a bad profession. If you succeed there are many rewards; if you disgrace yourself you can always write a book.

RONALD REAGAN, FORTIETH U.S. PRESIDENT (1911–)

2

Politicians

Advertising men and politicians are dangerous if they are separated. Together they are diabolical.

PHILLIP ADAMS, AUSTRALIAN COMMENTATOR AND BROADCASTER (1930–)

We hang the petty thieves and appoint the great ones to public office.

AESOP, GREEK SLAVE AND FABULIST, (CA. 550 BC)

He's a politician. That's a notch below child molester.

WOODY ALLEN, FILMMAKER (1935–)
Annie Hall

Man is by nature a political animal.

ARISTOTLE, GREEK PHILOSOPHER (384–322 BC)

Under every stone lurks a politician.

ARISTOPHANES, GREEK PLAYWRIGHT (450–385 BC)

The politician is an acrobat. He keeps his balance by saying the opposite of what he does.

MAURICE BARRÈS, FRENCH AUTHOR AND POLITICIAN (1862–1923)

Asking politicians to vote themselves out of power is like asking rabbits not to multiply; it ain't natural.

BOB BECKEL, POLITICAL CONSULTANT, ON TERM LIMITS (1949–)

Government is too big and too important to be left to the politicians.

CHESTER BOWLES, AMERICAN ADVERTISING EXECUTIVE AND POLITICIAN (1901–1986)

A bureaucrat is a Democrat who holds some office that a Republican wants.

ALBEN W. BARKLEY, U.S. VICE PRESIDENT (1877–1956)

It's a very good question, very direct, and I'm not going to answer it.

GEORGE H.W. BUSH, FORTY-FIRST U.S. PRESIDENT (1925–)

An honest politician is one who, when he is bought, will stay bought.

SIMON CAMERON, AMERICAN POLITICAL BOSS AND CABINET MEMBER (1799–1889)

There's nothing wrong with having a big ego. It's all right to have a Rolls Royce ego so long as you don't have a bicycle brain.

REV. JESSE JACKSON, CIVIL RIGHTS LEADER (1941–)

Politicians neither love nor hate. Interest, not sentiment, directs them.

LORD CHESTERFIELD, ENGLISH POLITICIAN (1694–1773)

I could have stayed home and baked cookies and had teas. But what I decided was to fulfill my profession, which I entered before my husband was in public life.

HILLARY RODHAM CLINTON, DEMOCRATIC SENATOR OF NEW YORK (1947–)

Politicians should read science fiction, not westerns and detective stories.

ARTHUR C. CLARKE, AUTHOR (1917–)

I've got all of my enemies here in the Cabinet where I can keep an eye on them.

JOHN DIEFENBAKER, CANADIAN POLITICIAN AND PRIME MINISTER (1895–1979)

People expect Byzantine, Machiavellian logic from politicians. But the truth is simple. Trial lawyers learn a good rule: "Don't decide what you don't have to decide." That's not evasion, it's wisdom.

MARIO CUOMO, FORMER DEMOCRATIC GOVERNOR OF NEW YORK (1932–)

What is inherently wrong with the word "politician" if the fellow has devoted his life to holding public office and trying to do something for his people?

RICHARD J. DALEY, FORMER CHICAGO MAYOR (1902–1976)

What this country needs is more unemployed politicians.

ANGELA DAVIS, AMERICAN POLITICAL ACTIVIST AND AUTHOR (1944–)

The world is weary of statesmen whom democracy has degraded into politicians.

BENJAMIN DISRAELI, BRITISH PRIME MINISTER (1804–1881)

Since a politician never believes what he says, he is quite surprised to be taken at his word.

CHARLES DE GAULLE, FRENCH GENERAL, STATESMAN, AND PRESIDENT (1890–1970).

Now I know what a statesman is; he's a dead politician. We need more statesmen.

BOB EDWARDS, NATIONAL PUBLIC RADIO HOST (1947–)

A leader in the Democratic Party is a boss, in the Republican Party he is a leader.

HARRY S. TRUMAN, THIRTY-THIRD U.S. PRESIDENT (1884–1972)

If a politician murders his mother, the first response of the press will likely be not that it was a terrible thing to do, but rather that in a statement made six years before, he had gone on the record as being opposed to matricide.

MEG GREENFIELD, POLITICAL COLUMNIST (1931–1999)

I have no trouble with my enemies. I can take care of my enemies in a fight. But my friends, my goddamned friends, they're the ones who keep me walking the floor at nights!

WARREN G. HARDING, TWENTY-NINTH U.S. PRESIDENT (1865–1923)

Patriotism is the last refuge of a scoundrel.

SAMUEL JOHNSON (1709–1784),
QUOTED IN *The Life of Johnson* BY JAMES BOSWELL

Mothers all want their sons to grow up to be president, but they don't want them to become politicians in the process.

JOHN FITZGERALD KENNEDY, THIRTY-FIFTH U.S. PRESIDENT
(1917–1963)

The only difference between the Democrats and the Republicans is that the Democrats allow the poor to be corrupt, too.

OSCAR LEVANT, AMERICAN PIANIST, COMPOSER, ACTOR (1906–1972)

Politicians are the same all over. They promise to build bridges, even where there are no rivers.

NIKITA KHRUSHCHEV, FORMER PRIME MINISTER, USSR (1894–1971)

Ninety percent of the politicians give the other ten percent a bad reputation.

HENRY A. KISSINGER, FORMER U.S. SECRETARY OF STATE (1923–)

History is replete with proofs, from Cato the Elder to Kennedy the Younger, that if you scratch a statesman you find an actor, but it is harder and harder, in our time, to tell government from show business.

JAMES THURBER, CARTOONIST AND HUMORIST (1894–1961)
"How to Tell Government from Show Business"

I once said cynically of a politician, "He'll doublecross that bridge when he comes to it."

OSCAR LEVANT, AMERICAN PIANIST, COMPOSER, ACTOR (1906–1972)

You have all the characteristics of a popular politician: a horrible voice, bad breeding, and a vulgar manner.

ARISTOPHANES, GREEK PLAYWRIGHT (450–388 BC)

In politics, nothing is contemptible.

BENJAMIN DISRAELI, BRITISH PRIME MINISTER (1804–1881)

Politicians talk themselves red, white, and blue in the face.

CLARE BOOTHE LUCE, AMERICAN PLAYWRIGHT, LEGISLATOR, AND DIPLOMAT (1903–1987)

That politician who curries favor with the citizens and indulges them and fawns upon them and has a presentiment of their wishes, and is skillful in gratifying them, he is esteemed a great statesman.

PLATO, GREEK PHILOSOPHER (427–347 BC)
The Republic

I don't make jokes. I just watch the government and report the facts.

WILL ROGERS, AMERICAN HUMORIST (1879–1935)

The most successful politician is he who says what the people are thinking most often in the loudest voice.

THEODORE ROOSEVELT, TWENTY-SIXTH U.S. PRESIDENT (1858–1919)

The Democrats are the party of government activism, the party that says government can make you richer, smarter, taller, and get the chickweed out of your lawn. Republicans are the party that says government doesn't work, and then get elected and prove it.

P. J. O'ROURKE, POLITICAL WRITER AND CRITIC (1947–)

A politician should have three hats. One for throwing into the ring, one for talking through, and one for pulling rabbits out of if elected.

CARL SANDBURG, AMERICAN POET (1878–1967)

We all know that prime ministers are wedded to the truth, but like other married couples, they sometimes live apart.

SAKI (H.H. MUNRO), BRITISH WRITER (1870–1916)

A conservative is a man with two perfectly good legs who, however, has never learned how to walk forward.

FRANKLIN DELANO ROOSEVELT, THIRTY-SECOND U.S. PRESIDENT (1882–1945)

An Independent is someone who wants to take the politics out of politics.

ADLAI STEVENSON FORMER, DEMOCRATIC GOVERNOR OF ILLINOIS AND U.S. AMBASSADOR TO THE U.N. (1900–1965)

Ninety-eight percent of the adults in this country are decent, hardworking, honest Americans. It's the other lousy two percent that get all the publicity. But then, we elected them.

LILY TOMLIN, COMEDIENNE (1939–)

A politician is a man who understands government. A statesman is a politician who's been dead for fifteen years.

HARRY S. TRUMAN, THIRTY-THIRD U.S. PRESIDENT (1884–1972)

Today's public figures can no longer write their own speeches or books, and there is some evidence that they can't read them either.

GORE VIDAL, AUTHOR, COMMENTATOR, AND CRITIC (1925–)

Politicians are like diapers. They both need changing regularly and for the same reason.

UNKNOWN

The first requirement of a statesman is that he be dull.

DEAN ACHESON, FORMER U.S. SECRETARY OF STATE (1893–1971)

I'm not a politician and my other habits are good.

ARTEMUS WARD, AMERICAN HUMORIST (1834–1867)

I have long enjoyed the friendship and companionship of Republicans because I am by instinct a teacher, and I would like to teach them something.

WOODROW WILSON, TWENTY-EIGHTH U.S. PRESIDENT (1856–1924)

I've seen many politicians paralyzed in the legs as myself, but I've seen more of them who were paralyzed in the head.

GEORGE C. WALLACE, FORMER GOVERNOR OF ALABAMA (1919–1998)

I do not admire politicians; but when they are excellent in their way, one cannot help allowing them their due.

HORACE WALPOLE, ENGLISH WRITER AND ANTIQUARIAN (1717–1797)

The military don't start wars. Politicians start wars.

GENERAL WILLIAM WESTMORELAND, FORMER COMMANDER OF U.S. FORCES IN VIETNAM (1914–)

Every man who takes office in Washington either grows or swells, and when I give a man an office, I watch him carefully to see whether he is growing or swelling.

WOODROW WILSON, TWENTY-EIGHTH U.S. PRESIDENT (1856–1924)

If the Republicans will stop telling lies about us, we will stop telling the truth about them.

ADLAI STEVENSON, FORMER DEMOCRATIC GOVERNOR OF ILLINOIS AND U.S. AMBASSADOR TO THE U.N. (1900–1965)

There are numerous bugbears in the profession of a politician. First, ordinary life suffers. Second, there are many temptations to ruin you and those around you. And I suppose third, and this is rarely discussed, people at the top generally have no friends.

BORIS YELTSIN, RUSSIAN PRESIDENT (1931–)

Politicians are people who, when they see light at the end of the tunnel, go out and buy some more tunnel.

SIR JOHN QUINTON, BRITISH BANKER AND POLITICAL CRITIC

A politician thinks of the next election; a statesman thinks of the next generation.

JAMES FREEMAN CLARKE, UNITARIAN MINISTER, SOCIAL REFORMER, AUTHOR (1810–1888)

A conservative is a man who sits and thinks, mostly sits.

WOODROW WILSON, TWENTY-EIGHTH U.S. PRESIDENT (1856–1924)

My choice early in life was either to be a piano player in a whorehouse or a politician. And to tell the truth, there's hardly any difference.

HARRY S. TRUMAN, THIRTY-THIRD U.S. PRESIDENT (1884–1972)

In politics, if you want anything said, ask a man; if you want anything done, ask a woman.

MARGARET THATCHER, FORMER BRITISH PRIME MINISTER (1925–)

3

Getting Elected

When the political columnists say "Every thinking man" they mean themselves, and when candidates appeal to "Every intelligent voter" they mean everybody who is going to vote for them.

FRANKLIN P. ADAMS, AMERICAN AUTHOR (1881–1960)

Vote: the instrument and symbol of a freeman's power to make a fool of himself and a wreck of his country.

AMBROSE BIERCE, AMERICAN AUTHOR AND SATIRIST (1842–1913)
The Devil's Dictionary

People never lie so much as after a hunt, during a war, or before an election.

OTTO VON BISMARCK, GERMAN CHANCELLOR (1815–1898)

Never interrupt your enemy when he is making a mistake.

NAPOLEON BONAPARTE, FRENCH GENERAL AND EMPEROR
(1769–1821)

I'll be glad to reply to or dodge your questions, depending on what I think will help our election most.

GEORGE H.W. BUSH, FORTY-FIRST U.S. PRESIDENT (1925–)

I would not vote for the mayor [of New York City]. It's not just because he didn't invite me to dinner, but because on my way into town from the airport there were such enormous potholes.

FIDEL CASTRO, CUBAN PRESIDENT-FOR-LIFE (1927–)

The problem with political jokes is they get elected.

HENRY CATE VII, AMERICAN POLITICAL OBSERVER

A troubled man for troubled times.

ALICE COOPER, SHOCK-ROCK STAR (1948–), ANNOUNCING HIS
INTENTION TO RUN FOR GOVERNOR OF ARIZONA

No part of the education of a politician is more indispensable than the fighting of elections.

SIR WINSTON CHURCHILL, BRITISH STATESMAN, PRIME MINISTER,
AND AUTHOR (1874–1965)

You campaign in poetry. You govern in prose.

MARIO CUOMO, FORMER DEMOCRATIC GOVERNOR OF NEW YORK
(1932–)

Get all the fools on your side and you can be elected to anything.

FRANK DANE, AMERICAN POLITICAL OBSERVER

To be a statesman, you must first get elected.

J. WILLIAM FULBRIGHT, FORMER DEMOCRATIC SENATOR OF ARKANSAS (1905–1995)

In order to become the master, the politician poses as the servant.

CHARLES DE GAULLE, FRENCH GENERAL, STATESMAN, AND PRESIDENT (1890–1970).

I offer my opponents a bargain: if they will stop telling lies about us, I will stop telling the truth about them.

ADLAI STEVENSON, FORMER DEMOCRATIC GOVERNOR OF ILLINOIS
AND U.S. AMBASSADOR TO THE U.N. (1900–1965), IN A 1952
CAMPAIGN SPEECH

The opposition is indispensable. A good statesman, like any other sensible human being, always learns more from his opponents than from his fervent supporters.

WALTER LIPPMANN, POLITICAL WRITER AND COLUMNIST (1889–1974)

In every election in American history both parties have their clichés. The party that has the clichés that ring true wins.

NEWT GINGRICH FORMER REPUBLICAN CONGRESSMAN OF GEORGIA
AND SPEAKER OF THE HOUSE (1943–)

A politician will do anything to keep his job, even become a patriot.

WILLIAM RANDOLPH HEARST, U.S. NEWSPAPER PUBLISHER
(1863–1951)

Half of the American people have never read a newspaper. Half never voted for President. One hopes it is the same half.

GORE VIDAL, AUTHOR AND CRITIC (1925–)

It's our fault. We should have given him better parts.

JACK WARNER, MOVIE MOGUL (1892–1978), ON HEARING THAT
RONALD REAGAN HAD BEEN ELECTED GOVERNOR OF CALIFORNIA

If a politician found he had cannibals among his constituents, he would promise them missionaries for dinner.

H.L. MENCKEN, AMERICAN JOURNALIST, EDITOR, ESSAYIST
(1880–1956)

While you're saving your face, you're losing your ass.

LYNDON BAINES. JOHNSON, THIRTY-SIXTH U.S. PRESIDENT
(1908–1973)

When we got into office, the thing that surprised me most was to find that things were just as bad as we'd been saying they were.

JOHN FITZGERALD KENNEDY, THIRTY-FIFTH U.S. PRESIDENT
(1917–1963)

I have been underestimated for decades. I have done very well that way.

HELMUT KOHL, GERMAN STATESMAN AND CHANCELLOR (1930–)

It is dangerous for a national candidate to say things that people might remember.

EUGENE MCCARTHY, FORMER DEMOCRATIC SENATOR OF MINNESOTA
(1916–)

It's easier to run for office than to run the office.

THOMAS P. "TIP" O'NEILL, FORMER DEMOCRATIC REPRESENTATIVE
OF MASSACHUSETTS AND SPEAKER OF THE HOUSE (1912–1994)

A lot of people voting for Pat Buchanan say they are doing so to send a message. Apparently that message is, "Hey, look at me, I'm an idiot."

DENNIS MILLER, COMEDIAN, TALK-SHOW HOST (1953–)

Spin is overrated. It is strategy, not spin, that wins elections.

DICK MORRIS, POLITICAL CONSULTANT (1949–)

The voters have spoken—the bastards.

RICHARD M. NIXON, THIRTY-SEVENTH U.S. PRESIDENT (1913–1994)

Although we may never know with complete certainty the identity of the winner of this year's presidential election, the identity of the loser is perfectly clear. It is the nation's confidence in the judge as an impartial guardian of the rule of law.

JOHN PAUL STEVENS, SUPREME COURT JUSTICE (1920–) ON THE 2000 ELECTION

The opposing party rarely causes so much angst as does one's own.

DICK MORRIS, POLITICAL CONSULTANT (1949–)

You can fool all the people some of the time, and some of the people all the time, but you cannot fool all the people all the time.

ABRAHAM LINCOLN (1809–1865)

Polling is merely an instrument for gauging public opinion. When a president or any other leader pays attention to poll results, he is, in effect, paying attention to the views of the people. Any other interpretation is nonsense.

GEORGE GALLUP, AMERICAN PUBLIC-OPINION ANALYST (1901–1984)

If voters don't have a stomach for me, they can get one of those blow-dried guys.

ROSS PEROT, PRESIDENTIAL CANDIDATE (1930–)

A low voter turnout is an indication of fewer people going to the polls.

DAN QUAYLE, FORTY-FOURTH U.S. VICE PRESIDENT (1947–)

There were so many candidates on the platform that there were not enough promises to go around.

RONALD REAGAN, FORTIETH U.S. PRESIDENT (1911–)

An election is a bet on the future, not a popularity test of the past.

JAMES "SCOTTY" RESTON, AMERICAN JOURNALIST (1909–1995)

The two real political parties in America are the Winners and the Losers. The people don't acknowledge this. They claim membership in two imaginary parties, the Republicans and the Democrats, instead.

KURT VONNEGUT, NOVELIST (1922–)

Decide on some imperfect Somebody and you will win, because the truest truism in politics is: You can't beat Somebody with Nobody.

WILLIAM L. SAFIRE, AMERICAN JOURNALIST, SPEECHWRITER (1929–)

Democracy: The substitution of election by the incompetent many for appointment by the corrupt few.

GEORGE BERNARD SHAW, IRISH PLAYWRIGHT (1856–1950)

The great thing about democracy is that it gives every voter a chance to do something stupid.

ART SPANDER, AMERICAN JOURNALIST (1939–)

It is enough that the people know there was an election. The people who cast the votes decide nothing. The people who count the votes decide everything.

JOSEPH STALIN, SOVIET DICTATOR (1879–1953)

In politics, stupidity is not a handicap.

NAPOLEON BONAPARTE, FRENCH GENERAL AND EMPEROR (1769–1821)

Get the facts first. You can distort them later.

MARK TWAIN, AMERICAN WRITER AND HUMORIST (1835–1910)

If you think too much about being re-elected, it is very difficult to be worth re-electing.

WOODROW WILSON, TWENTY-EIGHTH U.S. PRESIDENT (1856–1924)

There are many elements to a campaign. Leadership is number one. Everything else is number two.

BERND BRECHER, POLITICAL CONSULTANT (1933–)

I always voted for my party's call,
and I never thought of thinking for myself at all.
I thought so little, they rewarded me
By making me Ruler of the Queen's Navee!

W.S. GILBERT, ENGLISH LIBRETTIST (1836–1911) *HMS Pinafore*

If men were angels, no government would be necessary.

JAMES MADISON, FOURTH U.S. PRESIDENT (1751–1836)

I don't listen to any of them. Nobody has anything good to say.

CAROL EDBLOM, A SOUTH DAKOTA VOTER, ON NEGATIVE CAMPAIGN ADS

————•••————

You can fool some of the people all of the time, and those are the people you need to concentrate on.

ROBERT STRAUSS, DEMOCRATIC PARTY LEADER (1918–)

Everyone doesn't have a right to his opinion. The person who doesn't know what he's talking about does not have a right to his own opinion. It's why I'm never too much in favor of getting everyone out to vote on Election Day. Some people are too dumb or know too little about the issues and I hate to have one of them negating or canceling out the vote of someone who has bothered to inform him- or herself.

ANDY ROONEY, POLITICAL CRITIC (1919–), ON *60 Minutes*

A week is a long time in politics.

HAROLD WILSON, FORMER BRITISH PRIME MINISTER (1916–1995)

One of the penalties for refusing to participate in politics is that you end up being governed by your inferiors.

PLATO, GREEK PHILOSOPHER (427–347 BC)

It's no exaggeration to say that the undecideds could go one way or another.

GEORGE H. W. BUSH, FORTY-FIRST U.S. PRESIDENT (1925–)

Sometimes at the end of the day when I'm smiling and shaking hands, I want to kick them.

RICHARD M. NIXON, THIRTY-SEVENTH U.S. PRESIDENT (1913–1994)

If the Gods Had Meant Us to Vote, They'd Have Given Us Candidates

TITLE OF BOOK BY JIM HIGHTOWER (1943–)

—•—

The ballot is stronger than the bullet.

ABRAHAM LINCOLN (1809–1865)

Vote early and vote often.

JAMES MICHAEL CURLEY, FORMER MAYOR OF BOSTON (1874–1958)

———

Show me a good loser, and I'll show you a loser.

JIMMY CARTER, THIRTY-NINTH U.S. PRESIDENT (1924–)

———

When in doubt, tell the truth.

MARK TWAIN, AMERICAN WRITER AND HUMORIST (1835–1910)

I didn't say I wouldn't go into ghetto areas. I've been in many of them and to some extent I would say this: if you've seen one city slum, you've seen them all.

SPIRO T. AGNEW, FORMER U.S. VICE PRESIDENT (1918–1996), ON THE CAMPAIGN TRAIL

A citizen of America will cross the ocean to fight for democracy, but won't cross the street to vote in a national election.

BILL VAUGHAN, AMERICAN JOURNALIST (1915–1977)

Why pay money to have your family tree traced; go into politics and your opponents will do it for you.

UNKNOWN

———•••——

An election is coming. Universal peace is declared and the foxes have a sincere interest in prolonging the lives of the poultry.

T.S. ELIOT, POET AND ESSAYIST (1888–1965)

The United States brags about its political system, but the President says one thing during the election, something else when he takes office, something else at midterm, and something else when he leaves.

DENG XIAOPING, CHINESE LEADER (1904–1997)

You won't find average Americans on the left or on the right. You'll find them at Kmart.

ZELL MILLER, DEMOCRATIC SENATOR OF GEORGIA (1932–)

4

Power

Let them hate, so long as they fear.

LUCIUS ACCIUS, ROMAN PLAYWRIGHT (170–86 BC)

Under capitalism, man exploits man. Under socialism, it's just the opposite.

ANONYMOUS

Do not put such unlimited power into the hands of husbands. Remember all men would be tyrants if they could.

ABIGAIL ADAMS, WIFE OF SECOND U.S. PRESIDENT JOHN ADAMS (1744–1818)

A friend in power is a friend lost.

HENRY BROOKS ADAMS, U.S. HISTORIAN (1838–1918)

Power always thinks it has a great soul and vast views beyond the comprehension of the weak.

JOHN ADAMS, SECOND U.S PRESIDENT (1735–1826)

The price of power is responsibility for the public good.

WINTHROP ALDRICH, U.S. AMBASSADOR TO GREAT BRITAIN (1885–1974)

Power tires only those who do not have it.

GIULIO ANDREOTTI, FORMER ITALIAN PRIME MINISTER (1919–)

No Government can be long secure without a formidable Opposition.

BENJAMIN DISRAELI, BRITISH PRIME MINISTER (1804–1881)

Power is not revealed by striking hard or often, but by striking true.

HONORÉ DE BALZAC, FRENCH AUTHOR (1799–1850)

Numerous politicians have seized absolute power and muzzled the press. Never in history has the press seized absolute power and muzzled the politicians.

DAVID BRINKLEY, TV NEWSMAN (1920–)

A passion for politics stems usually from an insatiable need, either for power, or for friendship and adulation, or a combination of both.

FAWN M. BRODIE, BIOGRAPHER (1915–1981)

Those who have been once intoxicated with power, and have derived any kind of emolument from it, even though but for one year, never can willingly abandon it. They may be distressed in the midst of all their power; but they will never look to anything but power for their relief.

EDMUND BURKE, POLITICAL PHILOSOPHER (1729–1797)

If you must break the law, do it to seize power: in all other cases observe it.

JULIUS CAESAR, ROMAN GENERAL, STATESMAN, AND WRITER (100–44 BC)

You can get more done with a kind word and a gun than you can with a kind word alone.

ALPHONSE CAPONE, GANGSTER (1899–1947)

Victory has a hundred fathers, but defeat is an orphan.

GALEAZZO CIANO, MUSSOLINI'S FOREIGN MINISTER (1903–1944)

What we're saying today is that you're either part of the solution or you're part of the problem.

ELDRIDGE CLEAVER, BLACK PANTHER LEADER, CIVIL RIGHTS ACTIVIST, AUTHOR (1935–1998)

Real politics are the possession and distribution of power.

BENJAMIN DISRAELI, BRITISH PRIME MINISTER (1804–1881)

Power concedes nothing without a demand. It never did and it never will.

FREDERICK DOUGLASS, BLACK ABOLITIONIST, EDITOR, RENAISSANCE MAN (1818–1895)

Washing one's hands of the conflict between the powerful and the powerless means to side with the powerful, not to be neutral.

PAULO FREIRE, BRAZILIAN EDUCATOR AND PHILOSOPHER (1921–1997)

Political power grows out of the barrel of a gun.

MAO ZEDONG, CHINESE LEADER AND DICTATOR (1893–1976)

I came, I saw, I conquered.

JULIUS CAESAR, ROMAN GENERAL, STATESMAN, AND WRITER (100–44 BC)

I often say of George Washington that he was one of the few in the whole history of the world who was not carried away by power.

ROBERT FROST, AMERICAN POET (1874–1963)

Power doesn't corrupt people, people corrupt power.

WILLIAM GADDIS, AMERICAN AUTHOR (1922–1998)

There are two kinds of people, those who do the work and those who take the credit. Try to be in the first group; there is less competition there.

INDIRA GANDHI, INDIAN PRIME MINISTER (1917–1984)

The vice-presidency isn't worth a pitcher of warm spit.

JOHN NANCE GARNER, FORMER U.S. VICE PRESIDENT (1868–1967)

Whenever there is authority, there is a natural inclination to disobedience.

THOMAS C. HALIBURTON, CANADIAN JURIST AND HUMORIST (1796–1865)

The love of liberty is the love of others; the love of power is the love of ourselves.

WILLIAM HAZLITT, ENGLISH ESSAYIST AND CRITIC (1778–1830)

Strength lies not in defense but in attack.

ADOLF HITLER, GERMAN DICTATOR (1889–1945)

Power makes you attractive; it even makes women love old men.

JOSEPH JOUBERT, FRENCH PHILOSOPHER (1754–1824)

People say I am ruthless. I am not ruthless. And if I find the man who is calling me ruthless, I shall destroy him.

ROBERT F. KENNEDY, FORMER U.S. ATTORNEY GENERAL
AND DEMOCRATIC SENATOR FROM NEW YORK (1925–1968)

Power is the great aphrodisiac.

HENRY A. KISSINGER, FORMER U.S. SECRETARY OF STATE (1923–)

Power corrupts. Absolute power is kind of neat.

JOHN LEHMAN, FORMER U.S. SECRETARY OF THE NAVY (1942–)

Am I not destroying my enemies when I make friends of them?

ABRAHAM LINCOLN (1809–1865)

It is much more secure to be feared than to be loved.

NICCOLO MACHIAVELLI, ITALIAN STATESMAN AND POLITICAL
PHILOSOPHER (1469–1527).

All reactionaries are paper tigers. In appearance, the reactionaries are terrifying, but in reality they are not so powerful. From a long-term point of view, it is not the reactionaries but the people who are really powerful.

MAO ZEDONG, CHINESE LEADER AND DICTATOR (1893–1976)

What does not destroy me, makes me strong.

FRIEDRICH NIETZSCHE, GERMAN PHILOSOPHER (1844–1900)

There are no secrets to success. It is the result of preparation, hard work, and learning from failure.

COLIN POWELL, U.S. SECRETARY OF STATE (1937–)

He who pays the piper calls the tune.

PROVERB

I like power and I like to use it.

SAM RAYBURN, FORMER DEMOCRATIC CONGRESSMAN OF TEXAS AND
SPEAKER OF THE HOUSE (1882–1961)

Caesar had rather be first in a village than second at
Rome.

JULIUS CAESAR, ROMAN GENERAL, STATESMAN, AND WRITER
(100–44 BC)

There is a homely old adage, which runs: "Speak
softly and carry a big stick; you will go far."

THEODORE ROOSEVELT, TWENTY-SIXTH U.S. PRESIDENT (1858–1919)

Next to enjoying ourselves, the next greatest pleasure consists in preventing others from enjoying themselves, or, more generally, in the acquisition of power.

BERTRAND RUSSELL, BRITISH PHILOSOPHER (1872–1970)

The broad mass of a nation . . . will more easily fall victim to a big lie than to a small one.

ADOLF HITLER, GERMAN DICTATOR (1889–1945)
Mein Kampf

To be able to endure odium is the first art to be learned by those who aspire to power.

SENECA, ROMAN STATESMAN AND WRITER (5 BC–65 AD)

If absolute power corrupts absolutely, does absolute powerlessness make you pure?

HARRY SHEARER, AMERICAN ACTOR AND DIRECTOR (1943–)

Ideas are for more powerful than guns. We don't allow our enemies to have guns, why should we allow them to have ideas?

JOSEPH STALIN, SOVIET DICTATOR (1879–1953)

All the president is, is a glorified public relations man who spends his time flattering, kissing, and kicking people to get them to do what they are supposed to do anyway.

HARRY S. TRUMAN, THIRTY-THIRD U.S. PRESIDENT (1884–1972)

The way to have power is to take it.

WILLIAM MARCY "BOSS" TWEED, POLITICAL BOSS (1823–1878)

Character is power.

BOOKER T. WASHINGTON, AFRICAN-AMERICAN EDUCATOR
(1856–1915)

The illegal we do immediately. The unconstitutional takes a little longer

HENRY A. KISSINGER, FORMER U.S. SECRETARY OF STATE (1923–)

Mr. Churchill, Mr. Prime Minister, how many divisions did you say the Pope had?

JOSEPH STALIN, SOVIET DICTATOR (1879–1953)

———

Power is the perception of power.

THOMAS P. "TIP" O'NEILL, FORMER DEMOCRATIC CONGRESSMAN OF MASSACHUSETTS AND SPEAKER OF THE HOUSE (1912–1994)

———

There is no need to fear the strong. All one needs is to know the method of overcoming them. There is a special jujitsu for every strong man.

YEVGENI YEVTUSHENKO, RUSSIAN POET (1933–)

Politics gives guys so much power that they tend to behave badly around women. And I hope I never get into that.

BILL CLINTON, FORTY-SECOND U.S. PRESIDENT (1946–)

When spider webs unite, they can halt even a lion.

AFRICAN PROVERB

5

Foreign Affairs

How can you expect to govern a country that has two hundred and forty-six kinds of cheese?

CHARLES DE GAULLE, FRENCH GENERAL, STATESMAN, AND PRESIDENT (1890–1970)

Human rights is the soul of our foreign policy, because human rights is the very soul of our sense of nationhood.

JIMMY CARTER, THIRTY-NINTH U.S. PRESIDENT (1924–)

An appeaser is one who feeds a crocodile, hoping it will eat him last.

SIR WINSTON CHURCHILL, BRITISH STATESMAN, PRIME MINISTER, AND AUTHOR (1874–1965)

Our country: In her intercourse with foreign nations, may she always be right; but our country right or wrong.

COMMODORE STEPHEN DECATUR, AMERICAN NAVAL HERO (1779–1820)

You can always count on Americans to do the right thing—after they've tried everything else.

SIR WINSTON CHURCHILL, BRITISH STATESMAN, PRIME MINISTER, AND AUTHOR (1874–1965)

There are few ironclad rules of diplomacy but to one there is no exception. When an official reports that talks were useful, it can safely be concluded that nothing was accomplished.

JOHN KENNETH GALBRAITH, AMERICAN ECONOMIST AND AUTHOR (1908–)

Diplomat: A person who can tell you to go to hell in such a way that you actually look forward to the trip.

CASKIE STINNETT, WRITER, EDITOR, AND HUMORIST (1911–1998)
Out of the Red (1960)

When I am right, I get angry. Churchill gets angry when he is wrong. We are angry at each other much of the time.

CHARLES DE GAULLE, FRENCH GENERAL, STATESMAN, AND PRESIDENT (1890–1970)

I see little hope for a peaceful world until men are excluded from the realm of foreign policy altogether and all decisions concerning international relations are reserved for women, preferably married ones.

W. H. AUDEN, ANGLO-AMERICAN POET (1907–1973)
"PENIS RIVALRY," *A Certain World*

Sincere diplomacy is no more possible than dry water or wooden iron.

JOSEPH STALIN, SOVIET DICTATOR (1879–1953)

A man who does not know foreign language is igno-
rant of his own.

JOHANN WOLFGANG VON GOETHE, GERMAN WRITER, SCIENTIST
(1749–1832)

Whatever it is that the government does, sensible
Americans would prefer that the government do it to
somebody else. This is the idea behind foreign policy.

P.J. O'ROURKE, U.S. JOURNALIST (1947–)
"VERY FOREIGN POLICY," *Parliament of Whores* (1991)

I don't believe I'll ever get credit for anything I do in foreign affairs, no matter how successful it is, because I didn't go to Harvard.

LYNDON BAINES JOHNSON, THIRTY-SIXTH U.S. PRESIDENT
(1908–1973)

We are not afraid to entrust the American people with unpleasant facts, foreign ideas, alien philosophies, and competitive values. For a nation that is afraid to let its people judge the truth and falsehood in an open market is a nation that is afraid of its people.

JOHN FITZGERALD KENNEDY, THIRTY-FIFTH U.S. PRESIDENT
(1917–1963)

[The] American temptation [is] to believe that foreign policy is a subdivision of psychiatry.

ROBERT F. KENNEDY, FORMER U.S. ATTORNEY GENERAL AND
DEMOCRATIC SENATOR OF NEW YORK (1925–1968)

No foreign policy—no matter how ingenious—has any chance of success if it is born in the minds of a few and carried in the hearts of none.

HENRY A. KISSINGER, FORMER U.S. SECRETARY OF STATE (1923–)

The power of positive brinking.

ADLAI STEVENSON, FORMER DEMOCRATIC GOVERNOR OF ILLINOIS AND
U.S. AMBASSADOR TO THE U.N. (1900–1965), ON THE
DULLES–EISENHOWER FOREIGN POLICY

America is a large, friendly dog in a very small room.
Every time it wags its tail, it knocks over a chair.

ARNOLD TOYNBEE, BRITISH HISTORIAN AND PHILOSOPHER
(1889–1975)

This is the devilish thing about foreign affairs: they
are foreign and will not always conform to our whim.

JAMES "SCOTTY" RESTON, AMERICAN JOURNALIST (1909–1995)

Patriotism is often an arbitrary veneration of real estate above principles.

GEORGE JEAN NATHAN, AMERICAN EDITOR AND DRAMA CRITIC
(1882–1958)

Take the diplomacy out of war and the thing would fall flat in a week.

WILL ROGERS, AMERICAN HUMORIST (1879–1935)

Watching foreign affairs is sometimes like watching a magician; the eye is drawn to the hand performing the dramatic flourishes, leaving the other hand—the one doing the important job—unnoticed.

DAVID K. SHIPLER, PULITZER PRIZE-WINNING AUTHOR (1942–)

The principle of give and take is the principle of diplomacy—give one and take ten.

MARK TWAIN, AMERICAN HUMORIST AND WRITER (1835–1910)

My home policy: I wage war; my foreign policy: I wage war. All the time I wage war.

GEORGES CLEMENCEAU, FRENCH STATESMAN (1841–1929)

I'm convinced there's a small room in the attic of the Foreign Office where future diplomats are taught to stammer.

SIR PETER USTINOV, ACTOR, NOVELIST, PLAYWRIGHT, DIRECTOR (1921–)

Modern diplomats approach every problem with an open mouth.

ARTHUR J. GOLDBERG, LAWYER, DIPLOMAT, AND SUPREME COURT JUSTICE (1908–1990)

Treaties, you see, are like girls and roses; they last while they last.

CHARLES DE GAULLE, FRENCH GENERAL, STATESMAN, AND PRESIDENT (1890–1970)

It is our true policy to steer clear of permanent alliance with any portion of the foreign world.

GEORGE WASHINGTON (1732–1799), FAREWELL ADDRESS

All diplomacy is a continuation of war by other means.

ZHOU ENLAI, CHINESE COMMUNIST LEADER (1898–1976)

I wish that all Americans would realize that American politics is world politics.

THEODORE ROOSEVELT, TWENTY-SIXTH U.S. PRESIDENT (1858–1919)

Diplomacy is thinking twice before saying nothing.

UNKNOWN

If the United States of America or Britain is having elections, they don't ask for observers from Africa or from Asia. But when we have elections, they want observers.

NELSON MANDELA, SOUTH AFRICAN PRESIDENT, POLITICAL LEADER, NOBEL PRIZE WINNER (1918–)

From Stettin in the Baltic to Trieste in the Adriatic an iron curtain has descended across the Continent.

SIR WINSTON CHURCHILL, BRITISH STATESMAN, PRIME MINISTER, AND AUTHOR (1874–1965)

I traveled a good deal all over the world, and I got along pretty good in all these foreign countries, for I have a theory that it's their country and they got a right to run it like they want to.

WILL ROGERS, AMERICAN HUMORIST (1879–1935)

Foreign policy is really domestic policy with its hat on.

HUBERT H. HUMPHREY, U.S. DEMOCRATIC POLITICIAN, VICE PRESIDENT (1911–1978)

I asked Tom if countries always apologized when they had done wrong, and he says: "Yes; the little ones does."

MARK TWAIN, AMERICAN WRITER AND HUMORIST (1835–1910)
Tom Sawyer Abroad

In foreign policy you have to wait twenty-five years to see how it comes out.

JAMES "SCOTTY" RESTON, U.S. JOURNALIST (1909–1995)

Domestic policy can only defeat us; foreign policy can kill us.

JOHN FITZGERALD KENNEDY, THIRTY-FIFTH U.S. PRESIDENT (1917–1963)

6

The Presidency

A group of politicians deciding to dump a President because his morals are bad is like the Mafia getting together to bump off the Godfather for not going to church on Sunday.

RUSSELL BAKER, AMERICAN AUTHOR (1925–)

Anyone that wants the presidency so much that he'll spend two years organizing and campaigning for it is not to be trusted with the office.

DAVID BRODER, AMERICAN POLITICAL OBSERVER AND JOURNALIST (1930–)

You will be glad to know the President is practicing safe snacks.

LAURA BUSH, FIRST LADY, WIFE OF GEORGE W. BUSH (1946–), IN
REFERENCE TO HER HUSBAND'S FAINTING SPELL CAUSED BY A PRETZEL

I do not like broccoli. And I haven't liked it since I was a little kid and my mother made me eat it. And I'm President of the United States and I'm not going to eat any more broccoli.

GEORGE H. W. BUSH, FORTY-FIRST U.S. PRESIDENT (1925–)

CNN is one of the participants in the [Persian Gulf] war. I have a fantasy where Ted Turner is elected president but refuses because he doesn't want to give up power.

ARTHUR C. CLARKE, AUTHOR (1917–)

I had rather be right than be President.

HENRY CLAY, U.S. REPRESENTATIVE/SENATOR OF KENTUCKY (1777–1852)

I'm not going to have some reporters pawing through our papers. We are the president.

HILLARY RODHAM CLINTON, DEMOCRATIC SENATOR OF NEW YORK (1947–)

I've often wondered how some people in positions of this kind . . . manage without having had any acting experience.

RONALD REAGAN, FORTIETH U.S. PRESIDENT (1911–)

To be a great president, you have to have a war. All the great presidents have had their wars.

ADMIRAL WILLIAM CROWE, FORMER CHAIRMAN OF THE JOINT CHIEFS OF STAFF AND U.S. AMBASSADOR TO THE UNITED KINGDOM (1925–)

There they are. See no evil, hear no evil, and . . . evil.

BOB DOLE (1923–), FORMER REPUBLICAN SENATOR OF KANSAS AND PRESIDENTIAL NOMINEE, WATCHING FORMER PRESIDENTS CARTER, FORD, AND NIXON STANDING BY EACH OTHER AT A WHITE HOUSE EVENT

Do you realize the responsibility I carry? I'm the only person standing between Richard Nixon and the White House.

JOHN FITZGERALD KENNEDY, THIRTY-FIFTH U.S. PRESIDENT
(1917–1963)

When I was a boy I was told that anybody could become President; I'm beginning to believe it.

CLARENCE DARROW, AMERICAN LAWYER AND SOCIAL ACTIVIST
(1857–1938)

[President William] McKinley has no more backbone than a chocolate éclair!

THEODORE ROOSEVELT, TWENTY-SIXTH U.S. PRESIDENT (1858–1919)

Any man who wants to be president is either an ego-maniac or crazy.

DWIGHT DAVID EISENHOWER, THIRTY-FOURTH U.S. PRESIDENT (1890–1969)

There is nothing in the Constitution that authorizes or makes it the official duty of a president to have anything to do with criminal activities.

SAM ERVIN, FORMER DEMOCRATIC SENATOR OF NORTH CAROLINA, ON THE WATERGATE SCANDAL (1897–1985)

One of the little-celebrated powers of Presidents (and other high government officials) is to listen to their critics with just enough sympathy to ensure their silence.

JOHN KENNETH GALBRAITH, AMERICAN ECONOMIST AND AUTHOR (1908–)

Oh, that lovely title, ex-president.

DWIGHT DAVID EISENHOWER, THIRTY-FOURTH U.S. PRESIDENT
(1890–1969)

Things are more like they are now than they have
ever been.

GERALD FORD, THIRTY-EIGHTH U.S. PRESIDENT (1913–)

[The President is] the last person in the world to know what the people really want and think.

JAMES A. GARFIELD, TWENTIETH U.S. PRESIDENT (1831–1881)

———

I believe Moses was eighty when God first commissioned him for public service.

RONALD REAGAN, FORTIETH U.S. PRESIDENT (1911–)

We need a president who's fluent in at least one language.

BUCK HENRY, AMERICAN WRITER AND PERFORMER (1930–)

Many years ago, I concluded that a few hair shirts were part of the mental wardrobe of every man. The president differs from other men in that he has a more extensive wardrobe.

HERBERT HOOVER, THIRTY-FIRST U.S. PRESIDENT (1874–1964)

Anyone who thinks that the vice president can take a position independent of the president of his administration simply has no knowledge of politics or government. You are his choice in a political marriage, and he expects your absolute loyalty.

HUBERT H. HUMPHREY, U.S VICE PRESIDENT AND DEMOCRATIC SENATOR OF MINNESOTA (1911–1978)

———

At least she's the president of something, which is more than I can say.

BOB DOLE, FORMER REPUBLICAN SENATOR OF KANSAS AND PRESIDENTIAL NOMINEE, (1923–), ABOUT HIS WIFE ELIZABETH, PRESIDENT OF THE AMERICAN RED CROSS

I seldom think of politics more than eighteen hours a day.

LYNDON BAINES JOHNSON, THIRTY-SIXTH U.S. PRESIDENT
(1908–1973)

[Running for President is] physically, emotionally, mentally, and spiritually the most demanding single undertaking I can envisage unless it's World War III.

WALTER F. MONDALE, FORMER U.S. VICE PRESIDENT AND DEMOCRATIC
SENATOR OF MINNESOTA (1928–)

If one morning I walked on top of the water across the
Potomac River, the headline that afternoon would read
"President Can't Swim."

LYNDON BAINES JOHNSON, THIRTY-SIXTH U.S. PRESIDENT
(1908–1973)

When the president does it, that means it is not illegal.

RICHARD M. NIXON, THIRTY-SEVENTH U.S. PRESIDENT (1913–1994)

I know I'm not in government anymore. In fact I'm out of work.

RONALD REAGAN, FORTIETH U.S. PRESIDENT (1911–)

In our brief national history we have shot four of our presidents, worried five of them to death, impeached one, and hounded another out of office. And when all else fails, we hold an election and assassinate their character.

P. J. O'ROURKE, POLITICAL WRITER AND CRITIC (1947–)

Any American who is prepared to run for president should automatically, by definition, be disqualified from ever doing so.

GORE VIDAL, AUTHOR, COMMENTATOR, AND CRITIC (1925–)

Being president is like being a jackass in a hailstorm. There's nothing to do but stand there and take it.

LYNDON BAINES JOHNSON, THIRTY-SIXTH U.S. PRESIDENT (1908–1973)

There are blessed intervals when I forget by one means or another that I am President of the United States.

WOODROW WILSON, TWENTY-EIGHTH U.S. PRESIDENT (1856–1924)

Democracy means that anyone can grow up to be president, and anyone who doesn't grow up can be vice president.

JOHNNY CARSON, AMERICAN TELEVISION HOST (1925–)

I made my mistakes, but in all my years of public life, I have never profited from public service. I've earned every cent. And in all of my years in public life I have never obstructed justice. And I think, too, that I can say that in my years of public life that I welcome this kind of examination because people have got to know whether or not their President is a crook. Well, I'm not a crook. I've earned everything I've got.

RICHARD M. NIXON, THIRTY-SEVENTH U.S. PRESIDENT (1913–1994)

If Lincoln were alive today, he'd roll over in his grave.

GERALD FORD, THIRTY-EIGHTH U.S. PRESIDENT (1913–)

I think the presidency is an institution over which you have temporary custody.

RONALD REAGAN, FORTIETH U.S. PRESIDENT (1911–)

The election of a President is always to some extent a confession on the part of the public of its hopes and beliefs.

ANONYMOUS, WRITING AS "30-32"
High Low Washington

George Washington is the only president who didn't blame the previous administration for his troubles.

UNKNOWN

By the time a man gets to be presidential material, he's been bought ten times over.

GORE VIDAL, AUTHOR, COMMENTATOR, AND CRITIC (1925–)

I don't know whether it's the finest public housing in America or the crown jewel of the federal prison system.

BILL CLINTON, FORTY-SECOND U.S. PRESIDENT (1946–), ON THE WHITE HOUSE

In America, anybody may become president, and I suppose it's just one of the risks you take.

ADLAI STEVENSON, FORMER DEMOCRATIC GOVERNOR OF ILLINOIS AND U.S. AMBASSADOR TO THE U.N. (1900–1965)

7

Congress

You can't use tact with a Congressman! A Congressman is a hog! You must take a stick and hit him on the snout!

HENRY BROOKS ADAMS, AMERICAN HISTORIAN AND AUTHOR (1838–1918)

Oh! the wisdom, the foresight and the hindsight and the rightsight and the leftsight, the northsight and the southsight, and the eastsight and the westsight that appeared in that august assembly.

JOHN ADAMS, SECOND U.S. PRESIDENT (1743–1826), ON THE U.S. CONGRESS

No man is fit to be a Senator. . .unless he is willing to surrender his political life for great principle.

HENRY FOUNTAIN ASHURST, FORMER DEMOCRATIC SENATOR OF
ARIZONA (1874–1962)

Can any of you seriously say the Bill of Rights could get through Congress today? It wouldn't even get out of committee.

F. LEE BAILEY, HIGH-PROFILE DEFENSE ATTORNEY (1933–)

I would sooner live in a society governed by the first two thousand names in the Boston telephone directory than in a society governed by the two thousand faculty members of Harvard University.

WILLIAM F. BUCKLEY, JR., POLITICAL COLUMNIST
AND WRITER (1925–)

The House looks like more fun. It's like the Donahue show. The Senate is like one of those Sunday morning public service programs.

PHIL DONAHUE, TALK SHOW HOST (1935–)

It's just one big merry-go-round.

LARRY FLYNT, PUBLISHER OF *HUSTLER* MAGAZINE (1942–), ON THE
FREQUENCY OF AFFAIRS BETWEEN CONGRESSMEN AND INTERNS

An important antidote to American democracy is American gerontocracy. The positions of eminence and authority in Congress are allotted in accordance with length of service, regardless of quality. Superficial observers have long criticized the United States for making a fetish of youth. This is unfair. Uniquely among modern organs of public and private adminis-tration, its national legislature rewards senility.

JOHN KENNETH GALBRAITH, AMERICAN ECONOMIST AND
AUTHOR (1908–)

The idea that a congressman would be tainted by accepting money from private industry or private sources is essentially a socialist argument.

NEWT GINGRICH, REPUBLICAN FORMER OF CONGRESSMAN OF GEORGIA AND SPEAKER OF THE HOUSE (1943–)

The bottom line is, there have been a lot of nuts elected to the United States Senate.

CHARLES GRASSLEY, REPUBLICAN SENATOR OF IOWA (1933–)

The mistakes made by Congress wouldn't be so bad if the next Congress didn't keep trying to correct them.

CULLEN HIGHTOWER, HUMORIST (1923–)

We'd all like to vote for the best man but he's never a candidate.

KIN HUBBARD, AMERICAN POLITICAL HUMORIST (1868–1930)

The Senate is a place filled with goodwill and good intentions, and if the road to hell is paved with them, then it's a pretty good detour.

HUBERT H. HUMPHREY, U.S. VICE PRESIDENT AND
DEMOCRATIC SENATOR OF MINNESOTA (1911–1978)

There are so many women on the floor of Congress, it looks like a mall.

HENRY HYDE, REPUBLICAN REPRESENTATIVE OF ILLINOIS (1924–)

If the present Congress errs in too much talking, how can it be otherwise in a body to which the people send one hundred and fifty lawyers, whose trade it is to question everything, yield nothing, and talk by the hour?

THOMAS JEFFERSON, THIRD U.S. PRESIDENT (1743–1826)

There is but one way for a president to deal with Congress, and that is continuously, incessantly, and without interruption. If it is really going to work, the relationship has got to be almost incestuous.

LYNDON BAINES JOHNSON, THIRTY-SIXTH U.S. PRESIDENT (1908–1973)

The crime bill passed by the Senate would reinstate the Federal death penalty for certain violent crimes: assassinating the President; hijacking an airliner; and murdering a government poultry inspector.

KNIGHT-RIDDER NEWS SERVICE DISPATCH

Someone has said the best nursing home is the U.S. Senate.

ERNEST HOLLINGS, DEMOCRATIC SENATOR OF SOUTH CAROLINA (1922–)

We the people are the rightful masters of both Congress and the courts, not to overthrow the Constitution but to overthrow the men who pervert the Constitution.

ABRAHAM LINCOLN (1809–1865)

Congress is so strange. A man gets up to speak and says nothing. Nobody listens—and then everybody disagrees.

BORIS MARSHALOV, RUSSIAN VISITOR TO THE UNITED STATES IN 1907

The Senate is the last primitive society in the world. We still worship the elders of the tribe and honor the territorial imperative.

EUGENE MCCARTHY, FORMER DEMOCRATIC SENATOR OF MINNESOTA (1916–)

Every nation has the government it deserves.

JOSEPH DE MAISTRE, FRENCH DIPLOMAT, PHILOSOPHER (1753–1821)

We may not imagine how our lives could be more frustrating and complex—but Congress can.

CULLEN HIGHTOWER, HUMORIST (1923–)

Eighty percent were hypocrites, eighty percent liars, eighty percent serious sinners. . .except on Sundays. There is always boozing and floozing . . . I don't have enough time to tell you everybody's name.

WILLIAM "FISHBAIT" MILLER, CONGRESSIONAL DOORKEEPER (1989)

We trained hard, but it seemed that every time we were beginning to form up into teams, we would be reorganized. I was to learn later in life that we tend to meet any new situation by reorganizing; and a wonderful method it can be for creating the illusion of progress while producing confusion, inefficiency, and demoralization.

PETRONIUS ARBITER, ROMAN AUTHOR (CA. 210 BC)

The passion for office among members of Congress is very great, if not absolutely disreputable, and greatly embarrasses the operations of the Government. They create offices by their own votes and then seek to fill them themselves.

JAMES K. POLK, ELEVENTH U.S. PRESIDENT (1795–1849)

There are lots more people in the House. I don't know exactly—I've never counted, but at least a couple hundred.

DAN QUAYLE, FORTY-FOURTH VICE PRESIDENT OF THE U.S. (1947–), COMPARING THE HOUSE AND SENATE

I will not deny that there are men in the district better qualified than I to go to Congress, but gentlemen, these men are not in the race.

SAM RAYBURN, FORMER DEMOCRATIC CONGRESSMAN OF TEXAS AND SPEAKER OF THE HOUSE (1882–1961)

This country has come to feel the same when Congress is in session as when the baby gets hold of a hammer.

WILL ROGERS, AMERICAN HUMORIST AND WRITER (1879–1935)

Talk is cheap—except when Congress does it.

CULLEN HIGHTOWER, HUMORIST (1923–)

When they call the roll in the Senate, the senators do not know whether to answer "present" or "guilty."

THEODORE ROOSEVELT, TWENTY-SIXTH U.S. PRESIDENT (1858–1919)

Being elected to Congress is regarded as being sent on a looting raid for one's friends.

GEORGE F. WILL, POLITICAL COMMENTATOR (1941–)

What right does Congress have to go around making laws just because they deem it necessary?

MARION BARRY, FORMER MAYOR OF WASHINGTON, D.C. (1936–)

———

Reader, suppose you were an idiot. And suppose you were a Member of Congress. But I repeat myself.

MARK TWAIN, AMERICAN WRITER AND HUMORIST (1835–1910)

In your country club, your church, and business, about fifteen percent of the people are screwballs, light-weights, and boobs, and you would not want those people unrepresented in Congress.

ALAN SIMPSON, REPUBLICAN SENATOR OF WYOMING (1931–)

8

Washington, D.C.

The mystery of government is not how Washington works but how to make it stop.

P. J. O'ROURKE, AMERICAN HUMORIST AND WRITER (1947–)

You know what's interesting about Washington? It's the kind of place where second-guessing has become second nature.

GEORGE W. BUSH, FORTY-THIRD U.S. PRESIDENT (1946–)

People come to Washington believing it's the center of power. I know I did. It was only much later that I learned that Washington is a steering wheel that's not connected to the engine.

RICHARD GOODWIN, PRESIDENTIAL ADVISOR AND WRITER (1931–)

Washington is a city of Southern efficiency and Northern charm.

JOHN FITZGERALD KENNEDY, THIRTY-FIFTH U.S. PRESIDENT (1917–1963)

People only leave (Washington) by way of the box—ballot or coffin.

CLAIBORNE PELL, FORMER DEMOCRATIC SENATOR OF RHODE ISLAND (1918–1995)

Outside of the killings, Washington has one of the lowest crime rates in the country.

MARION BARRY, FORMER MAYOR OF WASHINGTON, D.C. (1936–)

Washington talks about herself, and about almost nothing else. It is about herself as the City of Conversation that she incessantly converses.

HENRY JAMES, AMERICAN AUTHOR (1843–1916)

It is sometimes called the City of Magnificent Distances, but it might with greater propriety be termed the City of Magnificent Intentions. . .Spacious avenues that begin in nothing and lead no where; streets, miles long, that only want houses, roads, and inhabitants; public buildings that need but a public to be complete.

CHARLES DICKENS (1812–1870), ON WASHINGTON, D. C.
American Notes

Washington was the one city in the east where any woman with money and talent could set up housekeeping and become an important hostess.

ALICE HOGE, AMERICAN AUTHOR
Cissy Patterson

If you want to have a friend in Washington, better buy a dog.

HARRY S. TRUMAN, THIRTY-THIRD U.S. PRESIDENT (1884-1972)

Corruption is no stranger to Washington; it is a famous resident.

WALTER GOODMAN, AUTHOR (1928–2002)

New York has total depth in every area. Washington has only politics; after that, the second best thing is white marble.

JOHN V. LINDSAY, FORMER NEW YORK MAYOR (1921–2000)

Whoever laid out Washington must have done it after a cocktail party.

SAM HUFF, FORMER WASHINGTON REDSKINS LINEBACKER (1934–)

Now NASA is on an unmanned space mission to the moon. I think NASA should redirect and have an unmanned space mission to Washington, D.C., and try to find out if there is any intelligent life left in the nation's capital.

JAMES TRAFICANT, FORMER DEMOCRATIC REPRESENTATIVE OF OHIO
(1941–)

Washington is a very easy city for you to forget where you came from and why you got there in the first place.

HARRY S. TRUMAN, THIRTY-THIRD U.S. PRESIDENT (1884–1972)

It's a tough town and the razor blades are invisible.

ARLEN J. SPECTER, REPUBLICAN SENATOR OF PENNSYLVANIA (1930–)

9

Democracy

I don't know exactly what democracy is. But we need more of it.

ANONYMOUS CHINESE STUDENT, DURING PROTESTS IN TIANAMEN SQUARE, BEIJING (1989)

The most radical revolutionary will become a conservative the day after the revolution.

HANNAH ARENDT, POLITICAL SCIENTIST AND PHILOSOPHER (1906–1975)

The most perfect political community is one in which the middle class is in control, and outnumbers both of the other classes.

ARISTOTLE, GREEK PHILOSOPHER (384–322 BC)
"POLITICS"

Vote for the man who promises least; he'll be the least disappointing.

BERNARD BARUCH, PRESIDENTIAL ADVISOR AND FINANCIER
(1870–1965)

To retain respect for sausages and laws, one must not watch them in the making.

OTTO VON BISMARCK, CHANCELLOR OF GERMANY (1815–1898)

Democracy is being allowed to vote for the candidate you dislike least.

ROBERT BYRNE, AMERICAN WRITER (1933–)

Man is the only animal that laughs and has a state legislature.

SAMUEL BUTLER, AMERICAN WRITER (1835–1902)

Don't you get the idea I'm one of those goddam radicals. Don't get the idea I'm knocking the American system.

ALPHONSE CAPONE, GANGSTER (1899–1947)

The best argument against democracy is a five-minute conversation with the average voter.

SIR WINSTON CHURCHILL, BRITISH STATESMAN, PRIME MINISTER, AND AUTHOR (1874–1965)

In a democracy, dissent is an act of faith.

J. WILLIAM FULBRIGHT, FORMER DEMOCRATIC SENATOR OF ARKANSAS (1905–1995)

My notion of democracy is that under it the weakest shall have the same opportunities as the strongest. . .no country in the world today shows any but patronizing regard for the weak. . .Western democracy, as it functions today, is diluted fascism. . .true democracy cannot be worked by twenty men sitting at the center. It has to be worked from below, by the people of every village.

MOHANDAS GANDHI [MAHATMA], INDIAN NATIONALIST AND SPIRITUAL LEADER (1869–1948)

If voting changed anything, they'd make it illegal.

EMMA GOLDMAN, ANARCHIST (1869–1940)

The price of freedom is eternal vigilance.

THOMAS JEFFERSON, THIRD U.S PRESIDENT (1743–1826)

Our democracy is but a name. We vote? What does that mean? It means that we choose between two bodies of real, though not avowed, autocrats. We choose between Tweedledum and Tweedledee.

HELEN KELLER, WRITER AND ACTIVIST FOR THE DISABLED (1880–1968)

I believe we are on an irreversible trend toward more freedom and democracy—but that could change.

DAN QUAYLE, FORTY-FOURTH U.S. VICE PRESIDENT (1947–)

Democracy is no easy form of government. Few nations have been able to sustain it. For it requires that we take the chances of freedom; that the liberating play of reason be brought to bear on events filled with passion; that dissent be allowed to make its appeal for acceptance; that men chance error in their search for the truth.

ROBERT F. KENNEDY, FORMER U.S. ATTORNEY GENERAL AND DEMOCRATIC SENATOR OF NEW YORK (1925–1968)

As I would not be a slave, so I would not be a master. This expresses my idea of democracy.

ABRAHAM LINCOLN (1809–1865)

In democracy everyone has the right to be represented, even the jerks.

CHRIS PATTEN, POLITICIAN AND EUROPEAN UNION COMMISSIONER (1944–)

Democracies are most commonly corrupted by the insolence of demagogues.

ARISTOTLE, GREEK PHILOSOPHER (450–385 BC) "POLITICS"

Democracy . . . is a charming form of government, full of variety and disorder; and dispensing a sort of equality to equals and unequals alike.

PLATO, GREEK PHILOSOPHER (427-347 BC) "THE REPUBLIC"

The most terrifying words in the English language are: I'm from the government and I'm here to help.

RONALD REAGAN, FORTIETH U.S. PRESIDENT (1911–)

It's not the voting that's democracy; it's the counting.

TOM STOPPARD, ENGLISH PLAYWRIGHT (1937–)

Democracy and socialism have nothing in common but one word, equality. But notice the difference: while democracy seeks equality in liberty, socialism seeks equality in restraint and servitude.

ALEXIS DE TOCQUEVILLE, FRENCH POLITICAL PHILOSOPHER (1805–1859)

Wherever you have an efficient government you have a dictatorship.

HARRY S. TRUMAN, THIRTY-THIRD U.S. PRESIDENT (1884–1972)

One voice is tiny, and alone it cannot be heard above the din of politics as usual. The people's voice, when it cries as one, is a great roar.

ROSS PEROT, BUSINESSMAN AND POLITICIAN (1930–)
United We Stand

Apparently, a democracy is a place where numerous elections are held at great cost without issues and with interchangeable candidates.

GORE VIDAL, AUTHOR AND CRITIC (1925–)

As Mankind becomes more liberal, they will be more apt to allow that all those who conduct themselves as worthy members of the community are equally entitled to the protections of civil government. I hope ever to see America among the foremost nations of justice and liberality.

GEORGE WASHINGTON (1732–1799)

In Italy for thirty years under the Borgias they had warfare, terror, murder, bloodshed—they produced Michelangelo, Leonardo da Vinci, and the Renaissance. In Switzerland they had brotherly love, five hundred years of democracy and peace and what did that produce. . .? The cuckoo clock.

ORSON WELLES, AMERICAN ACTOR AND DIRECTOR (1915–1985)

Democracy is the recurrent suspicion that more than half of the people are right more than half of the time.

E. B. WHITE, AMERICAN WRITER (1899–1985)

There can be no fifty-fifty Americanism in this country. There is room here for only hundred percent Americanism.

THEODORE ROOSEVELT, TWENTY-SIXTH U.S. PRESIDENT (1858–1919)

No man is good enough to govern another man without that other's consent.

ABRAHAM LINCOLN (1809–1865)

Democracy means simply the bludgeoning of the people by the people for the people.

OSCAR WILDE, IRISH PLAYWRIGHT AND AUTHOR (1854–1900)

Communism doesn't work because people like to own stuff.

FRANK ZAPPA, AMERICAN MUSICIAN (1941–1993)

Democracy is the art and science of running the circus from the monkey cage.

H.L. MENCKEN, AMERICAN ESSAYIST AND SOCIAL CRITIC (1880–1956)

The kind of government that is strong enough to give you everything you need is also strong enough to take away everything that you have.

RONALD REAGAN, FORTIETH U.S. PRESIDENT (1911–)

When the government fears the people, there is liberty. When the people fear the government, there is tyranny.

THOMAS JEFFERSON, THIRD U.S. PRESIDENT (1743–1826)

You can fool too many of the people too much of the time.

JAMES THURBER, WRITER AND CARTOONIST (1884–1961)

No man's life, liberty, or property is safe while the legislature is in session.

GIDEON J. TUCKER, NINETEENTH CENTURY NEW YORK LAWYER AND JUDGE

Democracy is when the indigent, and not the men of property, are the rulers.

ARISTOTLE, GREEK PHILOSOPHER (450–385 BC) "Politics"

A little rebellion now and then is a good thing.

THOMAS JEFFERSON, THIRD U.S PRESIDENT (1743–1826)

I regret that I have but one life to give for my country.

NATHAN HALE, REVOLUTIONARY WAR HERO AND MARTYR
(1755–1776), BEFORE BEING HANGED BY THE BRITISH

If a free society cannot help the many who are poor, it cannot save the few who are rich.

JOHN FITZGERALD KENNEDY, THIRTY-FIFTH U.S. PRESIDENT
(1917–1963), INAUGURAL ADDRESS (1961)

The genius of our ruling class is that it has kept a majority of the people from ever questioning the inequity of a system where most people drudge along, paying heavy taxes for which they get nothing in return.

GORE VIDAL, AUTHOR AND CRITIC (1925–)

It is perfectly true that that government is best which governs least. It is equally true that that government is best which provides most.

WALTER LIPPMANN, POLITICAL WRITER AND COMMENTATOR (1889–1974) *A Preface to Politics*

All this will not be finished in the first one hundred days. Nor will it be finished in the first one thousand days, nor in the life of this Administration, nor perhaps in our lifetime on this planet. But let us begin.

JOHN FITZGERALD KENNEDY, THIRTY-FIFTH U.S. PRESIDENT (1917–1963), INAUGURAL ADDRESS (1961)

10

Leadership

Each time someone stands up for an ideal, or acts to improve the lot of others, or strikes out against injustice, they send forward a ripple of hope.

ROBERT F. KENNEDY, U.S. ATTORNEY GENERAL AND FORMER DEMOCRATIC SENATOR OF NEW YORK (1925–1968)

You gain strength, courage, and confidence by every experience in which you really stop to look fear in the face.

ELEANOR ROOSEVELT, CIVIL RIGHTS LEADER AND HUMANITARIAN (1884–1962)

Ninety percent of leadership is the ability to communicate something people want.

DIANNE FEINSTEIN, DEMOCRATIC SENATOR OF CALIFORNIA (1933–)

———

You can have brilliant ideas, but if you can't get them across, your ideas won't get you anywhere.

LEE IACOCCA, AMERICAN BUSINESS LEADER (1924–)

Leadership is getting someone else to do what you want him to do because he wants to do it.

DWIGHT DAVID EISENHOWER, THIRTY-FOURTH U.S. PRESIDENT (1890–1969)

A leader is a dealer in hope.

NAPOLEON BONAPARTE, FRENCH LEADER AND EMPEROR (1769–1821)

Character is much easier kept than recovered.

THOMAS PAINE, REVOLUTIONARY WAR WRITER ON POLITICS
(1737–1809)

I not only use all the brains I have, but all I can borrow.

WOODROW WILSON, TWENTY-EIGHTH U.S. PRESIDENT (1856–1924)

Discontent is the first step in the progress of a man or a nation.

FORTUNE COOKIE QUOTE

A leader takes people where they want to go. A great leader takes people where they don't necessarily want to go but ought to be.

ROSALYNN CARTER, FORMER FIRST LADY (1927–)

If you don't say anything, you won't be called on to repeat it.

CALVIN COOLIDGE, THIRTIETH U.S. PRESIDENT (1872–1933)

I'm not the smartest fellow in the world, but I can sure pick smart colleagues.

FRANKLIN DELANO ROOSEVELT, THIRTY-SECOND U.S. PRESIDENT (1882–1945)

No one rises so high as he who knows not whither he is going. Not only strike while the iron is hot, but make it hot by striking. Do not trust the cheering, for those persons would shout as much if you or I were going to be hanged.

OLIVER CROMWELL, ENGLISH SOLDIER AND STATESMAN (1599–1658)

Only those who dare to fail greatly can ever achieve greatly.

ROBERT F. KENNEDY, FORMER U.S. ATTORNEY GENERAL AND
DEMOCRATIC SENATOR OF NEW YORK (1925–1968)

You're not to be so blind with patriotism that you can't face reality. Wrong is wrong, no matter who does it or says it.

MALCOLM X, AFRICAN-AMERICAN LEADER (1925–1965)

You must do the thing you think you cannot do.

ELEANOR ROOSEVELT, CIVIL RIGHTS LEADER AND HUMANITARIAN (1884–1962)

Authority doesn't work without prestige, or prestige without distance.

CHARLES DE GAULLE, FRENCH GENERAL, STATESMAN, AND PRESIDENT (1890–1970)

Freedom is about authority. Freedom is about the willingness of every single human being to cede to lawful authority a great deal of discretion about what you do.

RUDOLPH GIULIANI, FORMER MAYOR OF NEW YORK (1944–)

Now, I think that I should have known that he [John F. Kennedy] was magic all along. I did know it—but I should have guessed that it would be too much to ask to grow old with him and see our children grow up together. So now, he is a legend when he would have preferred to be a man.

JACQUELINE KENNEDY ONASSIS (1929–1994), AFTER HER HUSBAND'S ASSASSINATION

Sure it's a big job; but I don't know anyone who can do it better than I can.

JOHN FITZGERALD KENNEDY, THIRTY-FIFTH U.S. PRESIDENT (1917–1963)

The man whose first question, after what he considers to be a right course of action has presented itself, is "What will people say?" is not the man to do anything at all.

W. ARBUTHNOT LANE, BRITISH PHYSICIAN (1856–1943)

She would rather light a candle than curse the darkness, and her glow has warmed the world.

ADLAI STEVENSON, FORMER DEMOCRATIC GOVERNOR OF ILLINOIS AND
U.S. AMBASSADOR TO THE U.N. (1900–1965), ON LEARNING OF
ELEANOR ROOSEVELT'S DEATH IN 1962

Education makes people easy to lead, but difficult to drive; easy to govern, but impossible to enslave.

HENRY BROUGHAM, BRITISH STATESMAN (1778–1868)

First of all, let me assert my firm belief that the only thing we have to fear is fear itself—nameless, unreasoning, unjustified terror, which paralyzes needed efforts to convert retreat into advance.

FRANKLIN DELANO ROOSEVELT, THIRTY-SECOND U.S. PRESIDENT (1882–1945), 1933 INAUGURAL ADDRESS

There are two ways of spreading light: to be the candle or to be the mirror that reflects it.

EDITH WHARTON, AMERICAN NOVELIST (1862–1937)

As we are liberated from our own fear, our presence automatically liberates others.

NELSON MANDELA (1918–), SOUTH AFRICAN PRESIDENT, POLITICAL LEADER, AND NOBEL PRIZE WINNER

Nothing great will ever be achieved without great men, and men are great only if they are determined to be so.

CHARLES DE GAULLE, FRENCH GENERAL, STATESMAN, AND PRESIDENT (1890–1970)

A leader's role is to raise people's aspirations for what they can become and to release their energies so they will try to get there.

DAVID GERGEN, AMERICAN POLITICAL COMMENTATOR (1942–)

No man will make a great leader who wants to do it all himself, or to get all the credit for doing it. As I grow older, I pay less attention to what men say. I just watch what they do.

ANDREW CARNEGIE, INDUSTRIALIST AND PHILANTHROPIST
(1835–1919)

The art of leadership. . . consists in consolidating the attention of the people against a single adversary and taking care that nothing will split up that attention. . . The leader of genius must have the ability to make different opponents appear as if they belonged to one category.

ADOLF HITLER, GERMAN DICTATOR (1889–1945)

Leadership in today's world requires far more than a large stock of gunboats and a hard fist at the conference table.

HUBERT H. HUMPHREY, U.S. VICE PRESIDENT AND FORMER
DEMOCRATIC SENATOR OF MINNESOTA (1911–1978)

You're still the king—even in your underwear.

LUDWIG FULDA, GERMAN WRITER AND PLAYWRIGHT (1862–1939)

Be sure you are right, then go ahead.

DAVY CROCKETT, HUNTER AND FRONTIERSMAN (1786–1836).

We expect our leaders to be better than we are . . . and they should be or why are we following them?

PAUL HARVEY, AMERICAN NEWSCASTER (1918–)

Duty then is the sublimest word in our language. Do your duty in all things. You cannot do more, you should never wish to do less.

ROBERT E. LEE, CONFEDERATE ARMY COMMANDER (1807–1870)

The only man who never makes a mistake is the man who never does anything.

THEODORE ROOSEVELT, TWENTY-SIXTH U.S. PRESIDENT (1858–1919)

The first step in calculating which way to go is to find out where you are.

MARGARET THATCHER, FORMER BRITISH PRIME MINISTER (1925–)

It is an old adage that honesty is the best policy; this applies to public as well as private life, to States as well as individuals.

GEORGE WASHINGTON (1732–1799)

Some men are born mediocre, some men achieve mediocrity, and some men have mediocrity thrust upon them.

JOSEPH HELLER, AMERICAN WRITER (1923–1999)

There go the people. I must follow them for I am their leader.

ALEXANDRE-AUGUSTE LEDRU ROLLIN, FRENCH REVOLUTIONARY LEADER (1807–1874)

11

Money

When Bill Clinton blows his taxophone, America will be singing the blues.

GEORGE H.W. BUSH, FORTY-FIRST U.S. PRESIDENT (1925–)

It is the responsibility of the citizens to support their government. It is not the responsibility of the government to support its citizens.

GROVER CLEVELAND, TWENTY-SECOND AND TWENTY-FOURTH U.S. PRESIDENT (1837–1908)

The national budget must be balanced. The public debt must be reduced; the arrogance of the authorities must be moderated and controlled. Payments to foreign governments must be reduced, if the nation doesn't want to go bankrupt. People must again learn to work, instead of living on public assistance.

MARCUS TULLIUS CICERO, ROMAN ORATOR AND STATESMAN (106–43 BC)

The inherent vice of capitalism is the unequal sharing of blessings; the inherent virtue of socialism is the equal sharing of miseries.

SIR WINSTON CHURCHILL, BRITISH STATESMAN, PRIME MINISTER, AND AUTHOR (1874–1965)

The politicians don't just want your money. They want your soul. They want you to be worn down by taxes until you are dependent and helpless. When you subsidize poverty and failure, you get more of both.

JAMES DALE DAVIDSON, ENTREPRENEUR AND AUTHOR (1947–)

A billion here and a billion there, and soon you're talking about real money.

EVERETT MCKINLEY DIRKSEN, FORMER REPUBLICAN SENATOR OF ILLINOIS (1896–1989)

Companies come and go. It's part of the genius of capitalism.

PAUL O'NEILL, U.S. TREASURY SECRETARY (1935–), ON THE COLLAPSE OF ENRON

He that is of the opinion money will do everything may well be suspected of doing everything for money.

BENJAMIN FRANKLIN (1706–1790)

———

I have the most reliable friend you can have in American politics, and that is ready money.

PHIL GRAMM, FORMER REPUBLICAN SENATOR OF TEXAS (1942–)

Republicans believe every day is the Fourth of July, but Democrats believe every day is April 15.

RONALD REAGAN, FORTIETH U.S. PRESIDENT (1911–)

———

The man of power is ruined by power, the man of money by money, the submissive man by subservience, the pleasure seeker by pleasure.

HERMANN HESSE, GERMAN-SWISS WRITER (1877–1962)

A Republican would think the best part of Viagra is the fact that you could make money off of it.

JAY LENO, TELEVISION HOST (1950–)

Giving money and power to government is like giving whiskey and car keys to teenage boys.

P.J. O'ROURKE, AMERICAN HUMORIST, JOURNALIST (1947–)

Politics has become so expensive that it takes a lot of money even to be defeated.

WILL ROGERS, AMERICAN HUMORIST (1879–1935)

———

The things that will destroy America are prosperity at any price, peace at any price, safety first instead of duty first, the love of soft living and the get-rich-quick theory of life.

THEODORE ROOSEVELT, TWENTY-SIXTH U.S. PRESIDENT (1858–1919)

True individual freedom cannot exist without economic security and independence.

FRANKLIN DELANO ROOSEVELT, THIRTY-SECOND U.S. PRESIDENT
(1882–1945)

Endless money forms the sinews of war.

MARCUS TULLIUS CICERO, ROMAN ORATOR AND STATESMAN
(106–43 BC)

A government that robs Peter to pay Paul can always depend on the support of Paul.

GEORGE BERNARD SHAW, IRISH PLAYWRIGHT (1856–1950)

A liberal is a man who is willing to spend somebody else's money.

CARTER GLASS, FORMER U.S. SENATOR OF VIRGINIA (1858–1946)

Money alone sets all the world in motion.

PUBLILIUS SYRUS, ROMAN WRITER (46 BC–43 AD)

When I want to buy up any politicians I always find the anti-monopolists the most purchasable. They don't come so high.

WILLIAM H. VANDERBILT, RAILROAD BARON (1821–1885)

The art of government consists in taking as much money as possible from one class of the citizens to give to the other.

VOLTAIRE, FRENCH PHILOSOPHER (1694–1778)

Few men have virtue enough to withstand the highest bidder.

GEORGE WASHINGTON (1732–1799)

One man's wage increase is another man's price increase.

HAROLD WILSON, BRITISH PRIME MINISTER (1916–1995)

Prosperity is necessarily the first theme of a political campaign.

WOODROW WILSON, TWENTY-EIGHTH U.S. PRESIDENT (1856–1924)

Income tax returns are the most imaginative fiction being written today.

HERMAN WOUK, AMERICAN NOVELIST (1915–)

———————

I don't understand why someone would spend $2 million to get elected to a $125,000-a-year job. But they do it all the time.

JOSEPH NAPOLITANO, POLITICAL CONSULTANT

I just received the following wire from my generous Daddy [Joseph P. Kennedy]:
"Dear Jack. Don't buy a single vote more than necessary. I'll be damned if I'm going to pay for a landslide."

JOHN FITZGERALD. KENNEDY (1917–1963), THEN DEMOCRATIC SENATOR OF MASSACHUSETTS (1958)

Once the coffers of the federal government are opened to the public, there will be no shutting them again.

GROVER CLEVELAND, TWENTY-SECOND AND TWENTY-FOURTH U.S. PRESIDENT (1837–1908)

Blessed are the young, for they shall inherit the national debt.

HERBERT HOOVER, THIRTY-FIRST U.S. PRESIDENT (1874–1964)

The more corrupt the state, the more numerous the laws.

TACITUS, ROMAN HISTORIAN (55–120)

I'm proud to pay taxes in the United States; the only thing is, I could be just as proud for half the money.

ARTHUR GODFREY, AMERICAN RADIO AND TV PERSONALITY (1903–1983)

Some of you have money, while some are poor you know.
If you send me to Washington, I'll just divide the dough.

BETTY BOOP, 1930S FILM CARTOON HEROINE

Government's view of the economy could be summed up in a few short phrases: If it moves, tax it. If it keeps moving, regulate it. And if it stops moving, subsidize it.

RONALD REAGAN, FORTIETH U.S. PRESIDENT (1911–)

12

War

Be polite; write diplomatically; even in a declaration of war one observes the rules of politeness.

OTTO VON BISMARCK, CHANCELLOR OF GERMANY (1815–1898)

War is just a racket . . . It is conducted for the benefit of the very few at the expense of the masses.

SMEDLEY BUTLER, MAJOR GENERAL, USMC (1881–1940)

You cannot be President of the United States if you don't have faith. Remember Lincoln, going to his knees in times of trial in the Civil War and all that stuff.

GEORGE H. W. BUSH, FORTY-FIRST U.S. PRESIDENT (1925–)

War gives the right to the conquerors to impose any condition they please upon the vanquished.

JULIUS CAESAR, ROMAN GENERAL, STATESMAN, AND WRITER
(100–44 BC)

Those who can win a war well can rarely make a good peace and those who could make a good peace would never have won the war.

SIR WINSTON CHURCHILL, BRITISH STATESMAN, PRIME MINISTER, AND AUTHOR (1874–1965)

During war, the laws are silent.

MARCUS TULLIUS CICERO, ROMAN ORATOR AND STATESMAN (106–43 BC)

Well, if crimefighters fight crime and firefighters fight fire, what do freedom fighters fight? They never mention that part to us, do they?

GEORGE CARLIN, AMERICAN COMEDIAN (1937–)

We are not retreating—we are advancing in another direction.

DOUGLAS MACARTHUR, U.S. GENERAL AND MILITARY GOVERNOR OF JAPAN (1880–1964)

The great questions of the day will be decided not by speeches and majority votes . . . but by blood and iron.

OTTO VON BISMARCK, CHANCELLOR OF GERMANY (1815–1898)

I don't know what kind of weapons will be used in the third world war, assuming there will be a third world war. But I can tell you what the fourth world war will be fought with—stone clubs.

ALBERT EINSTEIN, THEORETICAL PHYSICIST AND PHILOSOPHER (1875–1955)

Politics and war are remarkably similar situations.

NEWT GINGRICH, REPUBLICAN FORMER CONGRESSMAN OF GEORGIA
AND SPEAKER OF THE HOUSE (1943–)

No real social change has ever been brought about without a revolution . . . revolution is but thought carried into action.

EMMA GOLDMAN, ANARCHIST (1869–1940)

Older men declare war. But it is youth who must fight and die.

HERBERT HOOVER, THIRTY-FIRST U.S. PRESIDENT (1874–1964)

———•••———

The only winner in the War of 1812 was Tchaikovsky.

SOLOMON SHORT

Patriotism is the willingness to kill and be killed for trivial reasons.

BERTRAND RUSSELL, BRITISH POLITICAL PHILOSOPHER (1872–1970)

You'll never have a quiet world till you knock the patriotism out of the human race.

GEORGE BERNARD SHAW, IRISH PLAYWRIGHT (1856–1950)

The greatest happiness is to scatter your enemy, to drive him before you, to see his cities reduced to ashes, to see those who love him shrouded in tears, and to gather into your bosom his wives and daughters.

GENGHIS KHAN, MONGOL WARLORD (1167–1227)

Mankind must put an end to war, or war will put an end to mankind.

JOHN FITZGERALD KENNEDY, THIRTY-FIFTH U.S. PRESIDENT (1917–1963)

I would say to the House, as I have said to those who have joined this Government: "I have nothing to offer but blood, toil, tears, and sweat."

SIR WINSTON CHURCHILL, BRITISH STATESMAN, PRIME MINISTER, AND AUTHOR (1874–1965), IN 1940

It doesn't require any particular bravery to stand on the floor of the Senate and urge our boys in Vietnam to fight harder, and if this war mushrooms into a major conflict and a hundred thousand young Americans are killed, it won't be U.S. senators who die. It will be American soldiers who are too young to qualify for the Senate.

GEORGE MCGOVERN, FORMER DEMOCRATIC SENATOR OF SOUTH DAKOTA AND PRESIDENTIAL NOMINEE (1922–)

Preparation for war is a constant stimulus to suspicion and ill will.

JAMES MONROE, FIFTH U.S. PRESIDENT (1758–1831)

War loses a great deal of its romance after a soldier has seen his first battle.

COLONEL JOHN S. MOSBY, CONFEDERATE GUERRILLA LEADER (1833–1916)

No poor bastard ever won a war by dying for his country. He won it by making other bastards die for their country.

GENERAL GEORGE S. PATTON, COMMANDER OF U.S. THIRD ARMY IN
WORLD WAR II (1885–1945)

"My country, right or wrong," is a thing that no patriot would think of saying except in a desperate case. It is like saying, "My mother, drunk or sober."

G. K. CHESTERTON, ENGLISH WRITER (1874–1936)

War is much too serious a matter to be entrusted to the military.

GEORGES CLEMENCEAU, FRENCH PRIME MINISTER (1841–1929)

———

When the tyrant has disposed of foreign enemies by conquest or treaty, and there is nothing to fear from them, then he is always stirring up some war or other, in order that the people may require a leader.

PLATO, GREEK PHILOSOPHER (427–347 BC)

When all is said and done, and statesmen discuss the future of the world, the fact remains that people fight these wars.

ELEANOR ROOSEVELT, AUTHOR, HUMANITARIAN, HUMAN RIGHTS LEADER (1884–1962)

A man may be a patriot without risking his own life or sacrificing his health. There are plenty of lives less valuable.

JAMES MELLON, WHO PAID $300 FOR A CIVIL WAR UNION ARMY DEFERMENT

We mean to hold our own. I have not become the King's First Minister in order to preside over the liquidation of the British Empire.

SIR WINSTON CHURCHILL, BRITISH STATESMAN, PRIME MINISTER, AND AUTHOR (1874–1965)

Decision makers in Washington must face the awkward and enduring fact that the sum of the total United States global interests and obligations is nowadays far greater than the country's power to defend them all simultaneously.

PAUL KENNEDY, AMERICAN HISTORIAN (1945–)

If there is not the war, you don't get the great general; if there is not a great occasion, you don't get a great statesman; if Lincoln had lived in a time of peace, no one would have known his name.

THEODORE ROOSEVELT, TWENTY-SIXTH U.S. PRESIDENT (1858–1919)

The tree of liberty must be refreshed from time to time with the blood of patriots and tyrants.

THOMAS JEFFERSON, THIRD U.S. PRESIDENT (1743–1826)

When the rich make war it's the poor that die.

JEAN-PAUL SARTRE, FRENCH WRITER, PHILOSOPHER (1905–1980)

Never advise anyone to go to war or to marry.

SPANISH PROVERB

Great empires are not maintained by timidity.

TACITUS, ROMAN SENATOR, ORATOR, SOLDIER (55–117)

Governments need armies to protect them from their enslaved and oppressed subjects.

COUNT LEO TOLSTOY, RUSSIAN WRITER (1828–1910)

If there is one basic element in our Constitution, it is civilian control of the military.

HARRY S. TRUMAN, THIRTY-THIRD U.S. PRESIDENT (1884–1972)

A great war always creates more scoundrels than it kills.

UNKNOWN

To be prepared for war is one of the most effectual means of preserving peace.

GEORGE WASHINGTON (1732–1799)

Whoever has an army has power, and war decides everything.

MAO ZEDONG, CHINESE LEADER AND DICTATOR (1893–1976)

Here is the answer which I will give to President Roosevelt. We shall not fail or falter; we shall not weaken or tire. Neither the sudden shock of battle nor the long-drawn trials of vigilance and exertion will wear us down. Give us the tools and we will finish the job.

SIR WINSTON CHURCHILL, BRITISH STATESMAN, PRIME MINISTER, AND AUTHOR (1874–1965)

I know [patriotism] exists, and I know it has done much in the present contest. But a great and lasting war can never be supported on this principle alone. It must be aided by a prospect of interest, or some reward.

GEORGE WASHINGTON (1732–1799)

Two thousand years ago the proudest boast was "civis Romanus sum." Today in the world of freedom the proudest boast is "Ich bin ein Berliner". . . . All free men, wherever they may live, are citizens of Berlin. And therefore, as a free man, I take pride in the words, "Ich bin ein Berliner."

JOHN FITZGERALD KENNEDY, THIRTY-FIFTH U.S. PRESIDENT
(1917–1963)

War is nothing more than the continuation of politics by other means.

KARL VON CLAUSEWITZ, PRUSSIAN MILITARY PHILOSOPHER
(1780–1831)

Now this is not the end. It is not even the beginning of the end. But it is, perhaps, the end of the beginning.

SIR WINSTON CHURCHILL, BRITISH STATESMAN, PRIME MINISTER, AND AUTHOR (1874–1965)

If only more of today's military personnel would realize that they are being used by the owning elite as a publicly subsidized capitalist goon squad.

SMEDLEY BUTLER, MAJOR GENERAL, USMC (1881–1940)

13

Quips and Philosophy

The greatest lesson in life is to know that even fools are right sometimes.

SIR WINSTON CHURCHILL, BRITISH STATESMAN, PRIME MINISTER, AND AUTHOR (1874–1965)

I have a simple philosophy. Fill what's empty. Empty what's full. Scratch where it itches.

ALICE ROOSEVELT LONGWORTH, DAUGHTER OF TEDDY ROOSEVELT AND WASHINGTON GRANDE DAME (1884–1980)

The best way to keep your word is not to give it.

NAPOLEON BONAPARTE, FRENCH LEADER AND EMPEROR (1769–1821)

Things may come to those who wait, but only the things left by those who hustle.

ABRAHAM LINCOLN (1809–1865)

You can put wings on a pig, but you don't make it an eagle.

BILL CLINTON, FORTY-SECOND U.S. PRESIDENT (1946–)

Patriotism is your conviction that this country is superior to all other countries because you were born in it.

GEORGE BERNARD SHAW, IRISH PLAYWRIGHT (1856–1950)

An enemy generally says and believes what he wishes.

THOMAS JEFFERSON, THIRD U.S. PRESIDENT (1743–1826)

It is a good thing for an uneducated man to read books of quotations.

SIR WINSTON CHURCHILL, BRITISH STATESMAN, PRIME MINISTER, AND AUTHOR (1874–1965)

I am not a member of any organized political party. I am a Democrat.

WILL ROGERS, AMERICAN HUMORIST AND WRITER (1879–1935)

A conservative is a liberal who was mugged the night before.

FRANK RIZZO, FORMER REPUBLICAN MAYOR OF PHILADELPHIA (1920–1990)

The one thing I do not want to be called is First Lady.
It sounds like a saddle horse.

Jacqueline Kennedy Onassis (1929–1994)

When a man says he approves of something in principle, it means he hasn't the slightest intention of carrying it out in practice.

Otto von Bismarck, chancellor of Germany (1815–1898)

A man can't be too careful in the choice of his enemies.

OSCAR WILDE, IRISH POET AND PLAYWRIGHT (1854–1900)

I would remind you that extremism in the defense of liberty is no vice. And let me remind you also that moderation in the pursuit of justice is no virtue.

BARRY GOLDWATER, FORMER REPUBLICAN SENATOR OF ARIZONA (1909–1998), ON ACCEPTING THE 1964 REPUBLICAN PRESIDENTIAL NOMINATION

A conservative is someone who makes no changes and consults his grandmother when in doubt.

WOODROW WILSON, TWENTY-EIGHTH U.S. PRESIDENT (1856–1924)

Republicans understand the importance of bondage between a mother and child.

DAN QUAYLE, FORMER U.S. VICE PRESIDENT (1947–)

I don't want to be charged with child abuse.

PAT BUCHANAN, WRITER AND PRESIDENTIAL CANDIDATE (1938–),
EXPLAINING WHY HE DID NOT CRITICIZE VICE PRESIDENT DAN QUAYLE

Once the toothpaste is out of the tube, it is awfully hard to get it back in.

H. R. HALDEMAN, PRESIDENTIAL ADVISOR (1926–1993),
ON THE WATERGATE REVELATIONS

This is the greatest concentration of talent and genius in this house except for those times when Thomas Jefferson ate alone.

JOHN FITZGERALD KENNEDY, THIRTY-FIFTH U.S. PRESIDENT (1917–1963), TO NOBEL PRIZE WINNERS AT A WHITE HOUSE DINNER

If one cannot catch the bird of paradise, better take a wet hen.

NIKITA KHRUSHCHEV, SOVIET PRIME MINISTER (1894–1971)

Too bad all the people who know how to run this country are busy running taxicabs or cutting hair.

GEORGE BURNS, AMERICAN COMEDIAN (1896–1996)

I say violence is necessary. It is as American as cherry pie.

H. RAP BROWN, POLITICAL ACTIVIST (1943–)

Put three Zionists in a room and they will form four political parties.

LEVI ESHKOL, FORMER ISRAELI PRIME MINISTER (1895–1969)

There cannot be a crisis next week. My schedule is already full.

HENRY KISSINGER, FORMER U.S. SECRETARY OF STATE (1923–)

If you want to get along, go along.

SAM RAYBURN, FORMER DEMOCRATIC CONGRESSMAN OF TEXAS
AND SPEAKER OF THE HOUSE (1882–1961)

If you can't stand the heat, get out of the kitchen.

HARRY S. TRUMAN, THIRTY-THIRD U.S. PRESIDENT (1884–1972)

Guidelines for bureaucrats: (1) When in charge, ponder. (2) When in trouble, delegate. (3) When in doubt, mumble.

JAMES H. BOREN, AMERICAN BUREAUCRAT (1925–)

Becoming a politician is the only step down I could take from being a journalist.

JIM HIGHTOWER, TEXAN, COLUMNIST, AND AUTHOR (1943–)

Patriotism is in political life what faith is in religion.

LORD ACTON, BRITISH WRITER AND HISTORIAN (1834–1902)
"NATIONALITY"

———•••———

Politics is my hobby. Smut is my vocation.

LARRY FLYNT, PUBLISHER OF *HUSTLER* MAGAZINE (1942–)

A hard dog to keep on the porch.

HILLARY RODHAM CLINTON, DEMOCRATIC SENATOR OF NEW YORK
(1947–), SPEAKING ABOUT HER HUSBAND

I've looked on many women with lust. I've committed
adultery in my heart many times. God knows I will do
this and forgives me.

JIMMY CARTER, THIRTY-NINTH U.S. PRESIDENT (1924–)

The main advantage of being famous is that when you bore people at dinner parties they think it is their fault.

HENRY A. KISSINGER, FORMER U.S. SECRETARY OF STATE (1923–)

I know only two tunes: one is "Yankee Doodle" and the other isn't.

ULYSSES S. GRANT, EIGHTEENTH U.S. PRESIDENT (1822–1885)

No one loves his country for its size or eminence, but because it's his own.

SENECA, ROMAN STATESMAN AND WRITER (5BC–65AD)

———

I have opinions of my own—strong opinions—but I don't always agree with them.

GEORGE H. W. BUSH, FORTY-FIRST U.S. PRESIDENT (1925–)

America did not invent human rights. In a very real sense, it is the other way around. Human rights invented America.

JIMMY CARTER, THIRTY-NINTH U.S. PRESIDENT (1924–)

Forgive your enemies, but never forget their names.

JOHN FITZGERALD KENNEDY, THIRTY-FIFTH U.S. PRESIDENT (1917–1963)

You cannot make a revolution with silk gloves.

JOSEPH STALIN, SOVIET DICTATOR (1879–1953)

Index

About the Author

William B. Whitman is a former diplomat with the U.S. Foreign Service who spent most of his career in Yugoslavia and Italy. Although he still travels extensively for the State Department, Bill now devotes much of his time to writing for magazines, including *Hemispheres, National Geographic Traveler,* and *The Robb Report.* He is also the author of *Washington, D.C: Off the Beaten Path* (Globe Pequot).